Copyright © 2021 Diego Marquez / Broken Film

All rights reserved. No part of this book may be reproduced, or stored in a retrieval system, or transmitted in any form or by any means, electronic, mechanical, photocopying, recording, or otherwise, without express written permission of the publisher.

This book is an unofficial work and the author is not associated with MGM or EON Productions. All consulted bibliography is cited except for passages from the original novels by Ian Fleming.

ISBN: 9798739902696

Cover design and Illustrations by: Mariana Necol
Edited by: Elisabeth Staak

COPYRIGHT NOTICE:

007 Gun Symbol Logo © 1962 Danjaq, LLC and United Artists Corporation. All Rights Reserved.
James Bond Gun Barrel Logo © 1988 Danjaq S.A. & MGM/UA.
James Bond Iris Logo © 1999 MGM Inc.
James Bond, 007 Gun Symbol Logo, and Other Bond-related Trademarks TM Danjaq, LLC.

Printed in the United States of America

THE BEST BOND

Why Nobody Does It Better Than Timothy Dalton

Diego Marquez

Broken Film

broken film

CONTENTS

Copyright
Title Page
Epigraph
Part I   1
Introduction   3
Understanding Fleming's Bond.   9
Part II   27
Sean Connery   28
George Lazenby   39
Roger Moore   52
Pierce Brosnan   63
Daniel Craig   75
Part III   89
Timothy Dalton   90
Conclusion   113
Endnotes   117
About The Author   121

It's very important to make the man believable so that you can stretch the fantasy. Whether people like this kind of Bond is another question.

TIMOTHY DALTON

PART I

INTRODUCTION

By the time of its release in 1995, *Goldeneye* had effectively saved the Bond franchise from certain death.

Following a six-year hiatus, development hell, and a drastically different political context thanks to the end of the Cold War, *Goldeneye* proved to audiences worldwide that James Bond was back, and that the franchise had a life beyond its original cultural and historical context. The film became a commercial success on release, grossing over $345 million worldwide; Making it the fourth biggest box office attraction of 1995, and the highest-grossing Bond film since 1979's *Moonraker*.

Many were the reasons for its success: Superb directing on behalf of Martin Campbell and a well-balanced story are only some of its high points, but what was considered at the time to be its true strength was the casting of Pierce Brosnan as James Bond.

Many film critics at the time underlined this fact. Writing for *The Chicago Sun-Times*, Roger Ebert praised Brosnan's performance as "sensitive" and "aware of his relationships" and an improvement over the character's previous portrayal, which he considered to be "cold and dispassionate." [1] A particularly interesting comment came from film critic James Berardinelli who described Brosnan as "a decided improvement over his immediate predecessor." [2]

One cursory glance at the critical reactions to Brosnan's portrayal of Bond will not fail to make an immediate comparison to the man who donned the shoulder holster before him: Timothy Dalton. In hindsight, the reaction is extreme, but back in 1995, it made perfect sense.

Dalton's two outings as Bond, 1987's *The Living Daylights,* and 1989's *Licence to Kill* were considered to be low points for the franchise. Dalton's performance was a dramatic shift for an audience used to twelve years of Roger Moore's comedic debonair Bond. The humor was severely toned down, and the violence and seriousness were ramped up in equal measures. The films dealt with very real geopolitical issues; From the Soviet occupation in Afghanistan to the boom of the Colombian drug cartels of the late eighties. Villains were not the usual cat-stroking evil geniuses with volcano lairs, they were very real people --with real-life proxies to boot--, and with painfully realistic motivations: Ones that differed greatly from the world-conquering antics of villains of yore.

Dalton was dry, dispassionate, cold, violent, and aggressive. An incredibly scathing review of *Licence to Kill* by Rick Groen for the Canadian newspaper *The Globe and Mail* sums up how acid the sentiment was regarding Dalton's two Bond outings:

> "[The filmmakers] have excised Bond from the Bond flicks; they've turned James into Jimmy, strong and silent and

(roll over, Britannia) downright American [...] the film is essentially Bond-less" 3.

    The negativity pervaded the box office as well. While *The Living Daylights* was a modest commercial success, *Licence to Kill* became the least financially successful entry in the franchise.

A lot of the blame for the failure was firmly placed on Dalton's shoulder, and when Brosnan finally succeeded him in 1994, the public and critics alike were eager to leave Dalton behind as merely an anomaly in the series, much like George Lazenby was considered in the late sixties.

    Fast-forward to the year 2006.

    Casino Royale, starring Daniel Craig in the role of James Bond, is released to unanimous critical and commercial acclaim. The film would eventually gross well over $600 million worldwide, making it the fourth highest-grossing film of 2006, and the highest-grossing Bond film since 2002's *Die Another Day*. Much like Brosnan with *Goldeneye*, the highest praise for *Casino Royale* was reserved for Craig's performance as Bond. For the first time in the franchise's history, realistic talk of a Bond performance to rival that of Sean Connery's became the standard of media buzz after the film's release; with most outlets frequently naming Craig as the best Bond of all time [4].

    Interestingly enough, the characteristics that critics and audiences alike praised Craig's Bond for are the same for which Dalton received much vitriol in the late eighties. Writing about *Casino Royale*, Roger Ebert praised Craig as "a superb Bond…

who gives the sense of a hard man…"; While *Timeout New York's* Joshua Rothkopf described Craig as "…a screwed-up Bond, a rogue Bond, a bounder, a scrapper…". Perhaps more interestingly --or egregiously, depending on how one looks at it-- *The Times* directly compared Craig's performance to that of Dalton's. What had changed after all these years?

As it happens, *a lot*.

The fact of the matter is that Dalton was not given the proper chance to prove his worth as a Bond actor. There is no doubt that the switch from the light-hearted Bond of the Moore era to the gritty coldness of the Dalton adventures did not click well with audiences from the get-go. Aside from that, the Bond producers were engaged in a fierce legal battle with MGM/United Artists for the safekeeping of the rights to the Bond franchise; Said legal battle would endure for the full duration of Dalton's contract as James Bond --effectively ending in 1994, the year Dalton walked out of the role and Brosnan was announced for *Goldeneye*--.

These are merely big-picture points concerning Dalton's tenure; There are other factors at play that clarify the context in which the perceived failure of Dalton's Bond operated. For example, we now know well enough that the reason *Licence to Kill* severely underperformed at the box office was a last-minute change in the marketing campaign on behalf of MGM. The crux of the marketing issue was the film's original title: *Licence Revoked*.

The title of the film --as well as the entire marketing campaign-- was completely scrapped and redone at the last minute to include a new approved title: *Licence to Kill*. The reasoning?: MGM feared that the *Licence Revoked* title would not go well with American audiences, since it is reminiscent of the common phrase for the withdrawal of a driving license [5].

The last-minute marketing change meant that *Licence to Kill* was severely under-marketed upon release; Something that proved to be deadly for the film's chances at the box office, given that it opened alongside *Lethal Weapon 2*, *Ghostbusters 2*, *Indiana Jones and the Last Crusade*, and the film that would eventually become the year's smash-hit: *Batman*. Unsurprisingly, *Licence to Kill* is the Bond film with the weakest US box-office performance of them all.

However, drastic tonal changes and marketing fiascos aside, the reality is that Dalton's performance was way ahead of its time. The key characteristic that maligned his Bond tenure is exactly the one aspect that was praised the most of Craig's Bond: The faithful adaptation to Fleming's original vision of the character.

Timothy Dalton's performance is the maximum expression of Ian Fleming's James Bond, a complete package encompassing the cold demeanor, the scalpel-like danger, and aggressiveness of the original character, as well as the elegance, panache, and physical description of Bond. It is exactly this completeness, depth, and faithfulness that renders Dalton's Bond --unlike both his predecessors and successors-- the most compelling and emotionally rich portrayal of the character on the big screen.

Throughout this book, we will take a look at Bond as written by its original creator. We will underline the vast differences between the cinematic and literary renditions of the character, and with an analytical eye for filmmaking and storytelling, we will compare and contrast Ian Fleming's Bond to his big-screen counterparts: Sean Connery, George Lazenby, Roger Moore, Pierce Brosnan, and Daniel Craig. Finally, we will take a comprehensive look at Timothy Dalton's Bond, and underline the vast overlap with Fleming's vision --and its effectiveness--.

For the sake of brevity and consistency, only the official films by EON Productions will be taken into account for this analysis, meaning that we will not examine 1967's *Casino Royale* and 1983's *Never Say Never Again*. This book also contains spoilers for all Bond films and Fleming novels.

UNDERSTANDING FLEMING'S BOND.

The James Bond franchise has become such a Behemoth in the film industry that people forget that Bond is a character rooted in the literary world.

It would not be a stretch to assume that the majority of the Bond audience has not read --or even is aware of-- the original Bond novels by Ian Fleming. This is unsurprising, as the last Fleming novel was released in 1966; And while the books continue to enjoy a respectable commercial run, it pales in comparison with the fifty-five-year-old multi-million dollar film franchise. It is especially difficult for the general audience to connect with Fleming's stories since the film adaptations have greatly departed from the Fleming plots as early as 1967's *You Only Live Twice.* As a consequence of this lack of exposure, it would be safe to say that the majority of that audience does not know the original characterization of James Bond.

Kickstarting the franchise with *Casino Royale* in 1953, Fleming crafted a unique mixture of escapism, masculine fantasy, and a surprisingly realistic set of plots and set pieces taken straight from World War II, during which Fleming served in Naval Intelligence for the British Royal Navy. The books were filled with generous doses of violence, sex, and --perhaps its most defining element-- adventure in the form of snobby high-society fantasy.

"A dry martini" Bond quips in *Casino Royale*, "Three measures of Gordon's, one of vodka, half a measure of Kina Lillet. Shake it very well until it's ice-cold, then add a large thin slice of lemon peel. Got it?" An iconic line delivered in the middle of a high-stakes baccarat game, in the most elegant casino in the South of France.

While being revolutionary and infinitely thrilling, the Bond novels are very much of their time in terms of customs and culture; Some of them can remain inaccessible for modern audiences. Many readers may find an issue with the racial comments in *Live and Let Die*, and a majority of them would struggle to follow the *chemin-de-fer* game in *Casino Royale* --given that Baccarat has progressively fallen out of favor as a stock-standard casino card game--.

However, a reason new readers may find the Bond novels difficult to engage with rests in the character of Bond itself.

There is no doubt that people that have grown up with the cinematic Bond will experience a slight sense of dissonance and surprise when encountering Fleming's creation. Those who favor Sean Connery's portrayal may find him a tad too cold. Perhaps the ones that favor Pierce Brosnan's Bond will be shocked at how emotionally unstable the character is --especially towards the end of the original Fleming series--, but at the same time those that favor

Daniel Craig will find Bond's emotional restraint odd; And all the Roger Moore fans will have no common ground to find at all.

Fleming's Bond is, in the most concise and reductive sense, a hitman wearing the guise of a hard-drinking, woman-loving, and emotionally unstable English spy. A cruel machine whose only humanity can be glimpsed through his internal monologue, especially when he tries his best to internalize his feelings. A perfect example being the end of *Casino Royale*, where his feelings after the suicide of Vesper Lynd --essentially the love of his life-- are quickly smothered by a simple yet cutting quip: "The bitch is dead". This comes, of course, after finding out that Vesper was a Russian spy.

This is not to say that the portrayals of Bond by the aforementioned actors are sub-par. It was a conscious decision by the filmmakers to take different approaches for Bond with every actor --it just so happens that with Dalton, they consciously decided to stick close to the books--.

At its core, we can distill the biggest differentiation between the cinematic Bond and the literary Bond into two categories: Control and coldness.

The cinematic Bond, for the most part, seems to be completely confident and in total control of any given situation. Even in life-or-death circumstances--where Bond is in the clutches of the villain--, the maximum reaction has always been preoccupied concentration. A big example of this can be seen in 1965's *Thunderball*:

Connery's Bond is shot by Fiona Volpe's henchmen as he

escapes their capture. The bullet manages to hit Bond in the leg as he enters the local Junkanoo parade to lose them. Despite having a bullet wound, there is no sign of any severe physical impairment or weakness on Bond's behalf, and even with a mild showing of pain by Connery, it does not become enough of an issue to disturb any sense of control he has; Once the scene ends, the wound stops being a thing altogether in the grand scheme of the film.

Now let us contrast that to a story decision that may shock newcomers to Fleming's Bond. In *Live and Let Die*, Bond is captured by Mr. Big in his Harlem base, and after an exchange between the two characters, the villain gives his henchman --Tee-Hee-- the order to "break the little finger of Mr. Bond's left hand." Fleming then writes the following lines:

> "The negro slowly unhinged the little finger of Bond's left hand, immovably bound to the arm of his chair. He held the tip between the finger and thumb and very deliberately started to bend it back, giggling inanely to himself. Bond rolled and heaved, trying to upset the chair, but Tee-Hee put his other hand on the chair-back and held it there. The sweat poured off Bond's face. His teeth started to bare in an involuntary rictus. Through the increasing pain he could just see [Solitaire's] eyes wide upon him, her red lips slightly parted. The finger stood upright, away from the hand. Started to bend slowly backwards towards his wrist. Suddenly it gave. There was a sharp crack."

Tee-Hee breaks Bond's finger, something that severely impairs and renders Bond fragile for two-thirds of the duration of the book. Only after he arrives in Jamaica --well into the third act of the story-- does the finger fully heal.

With the slight exemptions of 1999's *The World is Not Enough* and 2012's *Skyfall*, not a single Bond film has gone as far as to strip that much control from Bond away; And even in the aforementioned examples, the idea is not explored to its full extent. In *The World is Not Enough*, Bond suffers from a dislocated collarbone at the beginning of the film, but its purpose is to merely point out how knowledgeable the villain is of Bond; It is never used as either a plot element of suspense or character-building trait throughout the rest of the film.

Skyfall, however, does come closer to the spirit of the Fleming novels. At the beginning of the film, Bond is shot in the shoulder by Patrice in Istanbul, and this injury --along with his inactivity from field duty-- is used to create the sense that Bond may not be able to dominate every situation he finds himself in. The idea is not explored to its full extent --nor taken to the extremes of *Live And Let Die*'s broken finger-- as in the Fleming novels, but it is most definitely an instance of close proximity with the spirit of Fleming's Bond.

To cement this detachment between Fleming's Bond and the cinematic Bond, we can take a look at how this exact scene with Mr. Big is played out in the film adaptation of *Live And Let Die*.

Facing the exact threat of having his finger broken by Tee-Hee, Moore's Bond never exhibits the "rolling and heaving" described in the Fleming original, nor the involuntary rictus of his teeth. He remains preoccupied at best and slightly nervous at worst. Moore still delivers confidence and control despite the imminent physical danger. The scene is resolved without Tee-Hee breaking the finger.

Another fantastic example of how Fleming detaches Bond from having total control can be found --once again-- towards the end of *Live and Let Die*.

Mr. Big has tied Bond and Solitaire together and is intending to keelhaul the pair over a reef, where they would essentially be skinned alive and become bait for sharks and barracuda. Right before they are thrown into the water, Fleming writes the following lines:

> *"If they were still alive when the first shark's fin showed on the surface behind them Bond had coldly decided to drown Solitaire. Drown her by twisting her body under his and holding her there. Then he would try and drown himself by twisting her dead body back over to keep his under."*

Can one picture Bond as portrayed by Roger Moore, Pierce Brosnan, or even Sean Connery being capable of arriving at such a cold conclusion for himself and the Bond girl? Can one even picture a cinematic portrayal of Bond being put in a situation where he is stripped of any control whatsoever? In a way, we do have an answer, since this scene did appear in 1981's *For Your Eyes Only*.

Villain Aristotle Kristatos has tied Melina Havelock and Bond in order to keelhaul them. Essentially the same setup as in Fleming's novel, but with vastly different executions. Whereas Fleming's Bond has been stripped from all control and is ready to carry out such a cold act, Moore's Bond seems only mildly concerned at his predicament, and always projects a demeanor suggesting that he is in total control. In *Live And Let Die*, the problem is resolved thanks to a limpet mine that Bond had previously placed on Mr. Big's yacht --one that even by this point, Bond is convinced has completely failed or malfunctioned--. In *For Your Eyes Only*, Moore manages to break free from the rope by using an underwater rock to snap it from Kristatos' yacht. Both situations narratively serve their purpose given their position inside the story --In *Live and Let Die* it is the ending, while in *For Your Eyes Only* it is in the middle of the film--, but they give vastly different portrayals of the character of James Bond.

One of the most common criticisms that the Bond film franchise has received over the years is that Bond himself is portrayed almost as a superhero; Barely preoccupied or even affected by the do-or-die life-threatening situations he constantly finds himself in. Always cool, calm, and collected when faced with certain death --and even the death of his companions or friends--.

This concept of the hero as an in-control and powerful figure was in no doubt effective in the early sixties when the character first made its ripples in popular culture with Sean Connery. But over time --and as the films would settle down to a more pre-established formula--, diminishing returns would wear off on the general public.

Contributing to this is also the gradual genre transition of the Bond films from a balanced mix of spy-fi and hard-espionage to outright action-adventure. While the stunts and the action became more daring and spectacular, the narrative stakes sometimes would not be ramped up accordingly. After all, the thrill of action films is seeing *how* exactly the hero overcomes adversity, not necessarily *if* they would do so.

The problem for Bond becomes the fact that oftentimes there are not many moments of weaknesses in the action, and when there are, the situation is quickly solved by a gadget --which while a trademark of the film franchise, has the unintended effect of lessening the impact the character has on the action--. Not many moments abound where pure wit and improvisation get Bond out of trouble.

This is not to say that the gadgetry is always used to the detriment of the narrative. Perhaps the best inclusion of a Bond gadget is present during Red Grant's confrontation with Bond in the 1963 adaptation of *From Russia With Love*.

Throughout the film, we see SPECTRE weave the plot to kill Bond and disgrace MI6, as well as Bond hitting the required beats in blissful ignorance. The confrontation is highly suspenseful because Red Grant has been presented throughout the film as the most in-control character in the narrative. In essence, Bond has mostly not been in control during the entire duration of the film; Everything happened the way it needed to happen because Grant was, as delivered gleefully by the character, his "guardian angel". This already configures the stakes of the showdown with Bond: The ruthless machine of SPECTRE has operated flawlessly up until now, what can Bond *do*?

Bond eventually gets the upper hand thanks to Grant falling foul of the gas bomb placed by Q branch in Bond's attache-case. But the gadget *does not* resolve the conflict, it merely grants Bond the opportunity to become equals with his counterpart. The ensuing battle is entirely Bond versus Grant without any interference whatsoever.

Conversely, this is not to say that the lack of gadgets guarantees a perfect pay-off to Bond's decisions in the action. One of the greatest examples of this being Bond's escape from the alligator farm in 1973's *Live and Let Die*.

As Moore's Bond is left to be eaten in a small mound in the middle of an crocodile-infested lake, he utilizes the magnet on his watch to attract a nearby boat. However, the boat itself is tied to shore, and therefore unable to move towards his location. This in of itself is a perfect setup for a narrative moment of weakness for Bond. By subverting the expectation of the gadget's role in the story, the audience immediately knows that Bond is in deep trouble, and has nothing but his wit to rely on. Bond eventually escapes by hopping over a series of conveniently-placed crocodiles to shore.

While the stunt is in itself impressive and dangerous, the audience's suspension of disbelief is stretched too thin to make the moment a properly satisfying pay-off. The convenient nature of the crocodile's positioning cheapens the otherwise brilliant setup. It is only the comedic nature of Moore's Bond performance that grants palatability to the scene.

This brings us to the second point of dissonance for new readers of Bond: the coldness.

While there is definitively more overlap here between Fleming's Bond and the cinematic Bond, not many of the films dive deep into the darker side of the character. Daniel Craig's portrayal does hit closer to this mark, but it mostly lacks the subtlety that characterizes Bond --more on this later--.

In Fleming's original characterization, Bond's attitude and

way of compartmentalizing his relationships with other people are borderline sociopathic. Notorious examples include the aforementioned smothering of his feelings towards Vesper Lynd and the decision to drown Solitaire. This is, of course, an in-universe symptom of being a secret agent in a high-stakes geopolitical context, and while cultural and societal sensibilities of the time influence the characterization, many characters like Mathis and Felix Leiter repeatedly emphasize --and mock-- Bond's cold demeanor.

"Surround yourself with human beings, my dear James..." says Mathis in a touching moment from *Casino Royale* "...they are easier to fight for than principles." A glaring example of this internalization of emotion can be found in Fleming's 1957 novel *From Russia With Love*.

Bond, Tatiana Romanova, and Darko Kerim are escaping Turkey and the Eastern Bloc on board the Orient Express. They are carrying with them a Soviet SPEKTOR machine, and are falling into a carefully orchestrated trap on behalf of the Soviets to assassinate Bond and humiliate the British Secret Service. At some point during the journey, Darko Kerim --the head of MI6's Istanbul section-- is found dead in his train compartment alongside the body of his assassin.

It is important to keep in mind that throughout the novel Bond has established a deep relationship with Kerim, one of mutual admiration and respect. And now, Bond sees the dead body of the man he spent so much time with during his stay in Turkey, essentially someone seen by Bond as a great man has vanished. Fleming describes Bond's thought process upon seeing the body:

> *"Bond listened to his imagination. It was like watching a film. The sleeping Darko, the man slipping quietly through*

the door, the two steps forward and the swift stroke at the jugular. Then the last violent spasm of the dying man as he flung up an arm and clutched his murderer to him and plunged the knife down towards the fifth rib..."

The violence of Bond's mental image serves as a telling glimpse of his emotional state; The violence of the scene fueling the violence of his own emotions. Fleming quickly continues, and in one brief --yet impactful-- sentence he provides a fleeting sense of Bond's sentimentality beginning to crack his mask:

"...This wonderful man who had carried the sun with him. Now he was extinguished. Totally dead..."

And before Bond can crack more and showcase his emotions to the outside world --especially to the Greek border officials present on the scene--, his cold, self-preservation instinct kicks in, and the moment is quickly internalized:

"...Bond turned brusquely and walked out of sight of the man who had died for him. He began, carefully, non-committally, to answer [the Official's] questions."

Much like with Vesper Lynd, Bond seems to be on the verge of showcasing his sentimentality, but he ends up swallowing every single moment of it. The coldness remains pervasive, even when faced with the death of a great friend or the death of the love of his life.

When contrasted to its screen counterpart in 1963's *From Russia With Love*, we most definitely get a certain coldness from Sean Connery's portrayal of Bond, but we fail to see the underlying emotion behind the hardened exterior. Connery's attitude is that of a man understanding that Kerim knew the risks that came with the job, and that therefore he should be professional enough to carry on with the assignment. This definitely can be applied to the feelings of Fleming's Bond, but any sense of emotional connection is lost in the performance altogether. The contradiction is not there; There is only the sense of duty, and that, unfortunately, makes for a flat performance at a key narrative point in the story.

The coldness that pervades Fleming's Bond gets pushed to its absolute limit in the ending of the 1963 novel *On Her Majesty's Secret Service*. Where Teresa Bond (née Di Vicenzo) is gunned down by Ernst Stavro Blofeld and Irma Bunt merely hours after her marriage to Bond. On the final page of the novel, Bond is woken up by a German police officer after having suffered a car crash thanks to the actions of Blofeld and Blunt:

> *"Bond turned towards Tracy. She was lying forward with her face buried in the ruins of the steering wheel. Her pink hand-kerchief had come off and the bell of golden hair hung down and hid her face. Bond put his arm around her shoulders, across which the dark patches had begun to flower…"*

Fleming's concise yet romantic language betrays Bond's feelings, the reference to the blood pouring and staining Tracy's clothes as dark patches that begin to "flower" being particularly disturbing in its bitter-sweetness; Bond is effectively observing history repeat itself: A woman he truly loved --in all seriousness the only one since Vesper Lynd--, once again lies dead in front of him. With too much emotion to bear, Bond still manages to restrain his true feelings in an almost macabre way:

> "He pressed her against him. He looked up at the young man and smiled his reassurance. 'It's alright' he said in a clear voice as if explaining something to a child. 'It's quite alright. She's having a rest. We'll be going on soon. There's no hurry. You see--' Bond's head sank down against hers and he whispered into her hair-- 'You see, we've got all the time in the world."

The inability for the reader to discern whether his actions are a product of shock or Bond's psychological self-defense mechanism --or a combination of both-- makes this moment the most haunting one of all the Flemings novels. It is important to note how we get the real sense that this tragedy is severely affecting Bond, but we never see any outward display of his emotions --i.e. crying, unbridled rage--.

 Let us quickly compare this scene from the Fleming book with its screen counterpart in 1969's *On Her Majesty's Secret Service*, as well as Daniel Craig's reaction to Vesper's death in 2006's *Casino Royale*.

 In the screen adaptation of the scene, George Lazenby's Bond comes across as exceedingly detached from the situation; It is impossible to determine whether this was a directorial decision or a byproduct of Lazenby's limited acting range. The potential sense of shock is present, but one cannot help but feel that Lazenby is projecting some sort of mild disappointment on the situation. In essence, Lazenby's Bond misses the mark by coming just short of the emotional range of Fleming's Bond.

Now let us take a look at an approximation of this scene in *Casino Royale*. After having betrayed Bond, Vesper decides to sacrifice herself knowing that she will be saving Bond in return. Bond manages to take her out of the sunk elevator from the collapsed Venice apartment building and tries to re-animate her, albeit unsuccessfully. Bond then resorts to kissing her, and immediately withdraws from her body in a violent burst of physical emotion; We also note that Bond's eyes are watery with tears as he tries to calm himself down.

There is no doubt that when compared to previous portrayals of Bond, Craig's performance does come close to a truly emotional and "human" Bond, but therein itself lies the problem: Whereas Lazenby's Bond barely misses the mark by being too detached, Craig overshoots it by projecting way too much outwards emotion over what just happened. Both versions are excellent in serving the individualized portrayals of the Bond character for both actors, but they both fail at being a faithful adaptation of the character.

By this point, it is completely pertinent to ask oneself: "How do you outwardly perform the inner monologue of a cold, detached, and gritty character?"; It is an excellent question and one that will help us eventually understand the masterfulness of Dalton's performance as Bond.

The answer does not lie exclusively within the actor's performance, but in the combination of how the script is written, the direction the producers and filmmakers wish to follow, and then -- eventually-- the performance itself. It is entirely possible --though difficult-- to perform this internal monologue, but at its base, the narrative needs to be anchored to thematic elements that serve the contradictions of the character.

Fleming has a moral and emotional throughline that is established in 1953's *Casino Royale* --and is absent for the majority of the films with the exceptions of Dalton and Craig-- that grounds said contradictions. It comes in the chapter named *The Nature of Evil*, where Bond --who has survived Le Chiffre's torture-- reveals to Mathis his intention to resign from the Secret Service. They then reflect on the changing nature of history and the moral relativity of espionage and the intelligence community:

> *"When one's young, it seems very easy to distinguish between right and wrong, but as one gets older it becomes more difficult. At school it's easy to pick out one's own villains and heroes and one grows up wanting to be a hero and kill the villains."*

Bond further explains that at the rapid pace of history, heroes and villains constantly change parts, and the ideas one fights for today may become the villains of tomorrow. He compounds his argument by drawing a comparison to his battle with Le Chiffre.

> *"...but when the hero Le Chiffre starts to kill the villain Bond and the villain Bond knows he isn't a villain at all, you see the other side of the medal. The villains and heroes get all mixed up."*

James Bond is not a hero, and even less so an inspirational figure. He is a man that uses violence and coercion for either personal reasons, or for what he believes is "right". This is the core of the emotional contradiction of the character, someone that tries to grapple with his humanity in circumstances where the showcase of said humanity is the worst of weaknesses. The high-society fantasy aspect is a key element in the contradiction since they are merely coping mechanisms for Bond's condition. How glamorous can a Vodka Martini be when it is being drunk consistently to drown out the sorrow of the character?

This contradiction is extended on a meta-level. Since this bleak and cynical subtextual examination of Bond --and the nature of espionage-- is presented by Fleming in a package of escapist fantasy. In a way, in seeking the pleasure of the spy fantasy, the reader inevitably comes across the inherent darkness of the job --much like Bond himself--.

This moral and emotional throughline that permeates most of Fleming's novels is absent in the majority of the Bond films; The overarching ground is the escapist fantasy alone. Once again, this is not to demean the importance, excellence, and entertainment value of the films, but it is to underline the perceived emotional blandness for which the franchise has been criticized, and how in the instances that they decide to get closer to Fleming's Bond, the performance falls flat --examples of this will be explored in coming chapters--.

So if the foundation of the story is the escapist fantasy alone, the script is going to explore this and create a narrative that will inevitably leave no space for the inherent emotional contradictions. Once this occurs, the director and the producers will follow the line that the story in the script calls for, and therefore, the performance will inevitably fall into that line. This is, for example, why Sean Connery's stoicism, when faced with the death of Aki in 1967's *You Only Live Twice,* falls flat, whereas Dalton's quick-but-concise reaction to Sharkie's death in 1989's *Licence to Kill* works -- more on this later--.

With this cursory glance at Fleming's original characterization of James Bond, we can understand the basics of what makes and drives the original character. We understand how cold and dispassionate Bond can be, even when dealing with the people dearest to him. We also see how Fleming was more than happy to place Bond in situations where he is not one-hundred percent in control; As well as how the cinematic interpretations of Bond have consistently shied away from this narrative tool. Now let us take a look at how Sean Connery, George Lazenby, Roger Moore, Pierce Brosnan, and Daniel Craig compare and contrast with the original Fleming character, before diving into Timothy Dalton's portrayal.

PART II

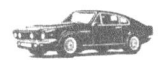

SEAN CONNERY

For many, Sean Connery's portrayal of James Bond remains the best one of the series --perhaps only rivaled by Daniel Craig--, and with very good reason.

Connery's Bond had a killer mix of elegance and danger in equal measures, where one could believe he could kill a man in cold blood in one minute, and make love to a beautiful woman the next. However, it is important to note that from the get-go of the Bond film franchise, producers Albert "Cubby" Broccoli and Harry Saltzman made the conscious decision to detach Connery's portrayal from Fleming's original vision, something revealed in an interview with "Cubby" Broccoli:

> *"It is important to understand that we never intended to play Sean Connery exactly as Fleming's Bond. The whole point about having Sean in the role, with his strong physical magnetism and the overtones of a truck driver, was that it thrilled the women, but, more important, young men in the audience could feel that there was a guy up there like them."* 6

So right from the beginning, we already have confirmation from the Bond producers themselves that the character was never intended to become a faithful adaptation of the Fleming original.

This in of itself does not necessarily pose a problem, nor mean that one can safely discard all Connery entries as valueless and trite. However, as it happens, the Connery films have the distinction of following the Fleming novels fairly closely --at least until 1967's *You Only Live Twice*--, and most of the plot situations do not mesh well with the directorial decisions regarding Connery's performance. The problem is, in essence, that the tension between what the story calls for and the distancing from Fleming's vision produce an un-nuanced Bond without the emotional contradictions that define the character.

In the previous chapter, we explored an instance of this differentiation when comparing Bond's reaction to Darko Kerim's death in both the novel and film version of *From Russia With Love*. For Connery's Bond, the job always comes first, and while the detached professionality of the character comes through well enough, we lack the emotional resonance to contradict it, thus robbing us of the true darkness of the character: The presence of the emotion and Bond's ability to suppress it are the key ingredients to the heart of the character. The emotional contradiction is everything.

Let us examine a non-Fleming example of Connery's Bond not displaying the nuance of the emotional contradiction in the 1967 film *You Only Live Twice*.

Bond --well into the process of turning Japanese-- survives

an attempted poisoning as he sleeps with his makeshift wife, Aki. While the assassin fails to eliminate Bond, he manages to successfully poison Aki, killing her almost instantly. Bond's reaction is so stoic that it, unfortunately, comes off as flat; The directorial and writing decisions severely handicapping the consistency of Connery's performance.

The objectively high-stakes setup of *You Only Live Twice's* plot, as well as the ruthlessness and pervasiveness of Blofeld and SPECTRE as villains, are diluted in the way Bond is handled both in the script and directorially. The plot setups call for what is essentially the most dangerous mission Bond has ever partaken -- a parallel drawn from the Fleming original--, but in keeping with the preconceived notion of Bond as the in-control distanced figure to Fleming's original, the payoffs feel off and --in the worst cases-- borderline parodical. All thanks to the detached coolness of Bond's portrayal.

The lack of emotional nuance in moments like these, even when dealing with minor or secondary characters, is not only a key aspect of Connery's Bond films but most subsequent films of the franchise. It is an unfortunate side effect of consciously not sticking close to Fleming's vision of Bond, and it prepared the context for the more outlandish and detached adventures to come.

Let us now see an example of Fleming's Bond dealing with the death of a secondary character/companion in the 1959 novel *Goldfinger*.

Bond teams up with Tilly Masterson to take down Auric Goldfinger. While Bond is doing so under orders of M, Tilly is doing so for personal reasons. She reveals to Bond that her sister Jill --Goldfinger's secretary and romantic fling for Bond at the beginning of the novel-- has been killed by Goldfinger's henchman Oddjob. This comes after her complicity with Bond in the ousting of Goldfinger as a card cheat. Jill is killed by skin suffocation after having her whole body painted in gold. Bond's reaction --as written by Fleming-- upon hearing the news from Tilly reveals his internal emotional turmoil:

> "Bond closed his eyes tight, fighting with a wave of mental nausea. More death! More blood on his hands. This time, the result of a careless gesture, a piece of bravado that had led to twenty-four hours of ecstasy with a beautiful girl who had taken his fancy and, in the end, rather more than his fancy [...]"

Once again, Fleming's succinct but impactful sentences pack a subtextual punch into very few lines. While the ghost of Vesper Lynd does keep haunting Bond, he has always remained open to emotional attachments to other women. It just so happens that whenever he lets himself open up, the realities of his life and job hit him hard. In his reality, no person is minor to him unless it is an underling of the enemy --and even then, it is merely a psychological defense mechanism to rationalize the violence he inflicts upon them--. It is of note how the only outwards display of this emotion is the closing of his eyes which is one of the few instances of physical display of his inner monologue. Fleming continues:

> " [...] By God, he'd pin this murder on Goldfinger if it was the last act of his life. As for himself...? Bond knew the answer. This death he would not be able to excuse as being part of his job. This death he would have to live with."

The anger and self-hatred --again, an instance of Bond not being in control-- are evident more than ever, the decision to "live with" Jill's death effectively dragging his assignment with Goldfinger beyond the professional boundaries of the job at hand and into a personal realm. If there is an emotion that Fleming's Bond is more in tune with than love, it is anger and hate; And he always channels his anger either toward the job at hand or --when he is off active field duty-- into drinking.

Of course, this reaction is a far cry from what we get from Connery in the 1964 film adaptation of *Goldfinger*. While there is no doubt that this is one of the few instances where we see Connery's Bond affected by what he's seeing, the range is limited.

To the film adaptation's credit, though, the long soiree onboard the train with Jill is obviated in favor of the more immediate image of her painted gold. But even if there is no narrative space to develop their relationship, the ensuing stoicism of Connery fails to deliver the other function of the moment in Fleming's original novel: Drive home the cruelty and sadism of Goldfinger's character --effectively elevating the narrative stakes--. Once again, the film plays the moment merely for the striking visual and the fantasy aspect and does not compound it more effectively to obvious implications of Goldfinger's demeanor as a villain.

Again, this is not to fault Connery himself for his performance, since his Bond --by design-- was intended to create a stoic, aspirational sex symbol. However, the matter-of-factness of the moment fails to fully compound what is essentially a striking and classic image.

To Connery's and the filmmaker's credit, they did manage

to create two successful overlaps between the cinematic portrayal of Bond, and Fleming's vision of the character, effectively providing great yet subtle emotional moments. These two instances provide the only moments where Connery's characterization of Bond becomes a one-to-one adaptation of the internal monologue of the Fleming original, and with graceful performances to boot.

The first can be found in 1962's *Dr. No*, in a scene not present in the original novel but written for the film. After failing to kill Bond with a tarantula, Professor Dent --one of Dr. No's minions-- retorts to shoot Bond as he is staying in the house of his secretary, Miss Taro. Dent eventually falls into a trap set up by Bond who holds him at gunpoint. After a brief exchange, Dent attempts to shoot Bond with his gun --depleted after emptying his ammunition in what he thought was the figure of Bond sleeping in a bed--. Bond then delivers one of the most iconic lines of the film franchise: "That's a Smith & Wesson, and you've had your six". Bond then proceeds to shoot Dent in cold blood.

What happens next is quick and subtle, but still impactful enough for us as an audience to register: Connery's Bond detaches the silencer from his Walther PPK, and as he blows the smoke out of the metal barrel, we get a glimpse of resignation --or maybe even sadness-- at the act he just committed.

The small pause after cleaning the silencer gives us a fleeting glimpse at Bond's internal monologue, essentially we see a paragraph of Fleming's writing in one second of acting: Bond is not happy with what he has done, and kills in cold blood such as this one chip at him in a grave way. The eventual internalization of his feelings, seen as the quick change of Connery's expression right before the scene fades out, underlines the emotional contradiction of the character.

The scene plays out to Connery's greatest strength as a Bond actor: the ability to project a professional detachment to the situations he is exposed to, but it does so by providing a counterpoint to this otherwise one-sided coldness. It is therefore a rare instance of Connery's Bond becoming a faithful adaptation of Fleming's original.

While this scene is not present in the original novel, we still get a moment in Fleming's *Dr. No* that informs us of Bond's attitude towards killing in cold-blood and the eventual rationalization for his actions. As he is escaping Dr. No's guano processing plant alongside Honey Rider, Bond manages to procure a gun, and they are eventually caught in a tunnel while an unsuspecting group of guards is approaching them: "I'm sorry, Honey." says Bond, "I'm afraid I'm going to have to kill them". Fleming then writes the following:

> "Bond knew he wasn't going to like this, killing again in cold blood, but these men would be the Chinese Negro gangsters, the strong-arm guards who did the dirty work. They would certainly be murderers many times over. Perhaps they were the ones who had killed Strangways and the girl. But there was no point in trying to ease his conscience. It was killed or be killed. He must just do it efficiently."

The cold-blooded killing does take a toll on Bond, but the emotional weight is reduced thanks to his capacity to compartmentalize and rationalize his actions. It is interesting to note that this is a case where we see Bond struggling to do so effectively. He begins by painting the coming guards as malevolent and brutish beings, he then tries to anchor the coming action in some sort of moral high ground by suggesting that the guards would be murderers many times over, and therefore their death would mean an overall moral gain in the world. Bond then brings it to a personal level by suggesting to himself that these people could be the killers of his dear friend Strangways and his secretary --the event that starts the plot of *Dr. No*--. When even that level of rationalization does not work, Bond takes it to the most primal of levels: kill or be killed.

This inherent conflict of the character, the toll of killing in cold blood, is present in the scene with Professor Dent in the film version of *Dr. No*. It is also an instance of script, filmmakers, and actors working in tandem towards a deeper characterization of James Bond. Compare this with the previously mentioned scene from *You Only Live Twice* --where Aki is killed--, and the difference is night and day.

The second instance of Connery's Bond becoming a one-to-one adaptation of Fleming's original characterization of James Bond is present in 1964's *Goldfinger*. It also turns out to be an odd moment where, despite being almost identical to its literary counterpart, the cinematic portrayal of Bond remains true and consistent to its character than what Fleming committed to the page. The moment in question is the death of Tilly Masterson at the hands of Oddjob.

In the novel, it occurs towards the end of the book as Goldfinger attempts to raid Fort Knox, while in the film it occurs halfway through the narrative, as Bond tries to spy on Goldfinger's Swiss refinery.

In the film version, Oddjob makes use of his deadly bowler hat to kill Tilly in a swift stroke. Bond --who has the option to keep escaping-- decides to go to where her dead body lays. Connery's initial reaction is superb in portraying not only dismay, but a sense that she died needlessly through his actions since he commanded her to run --a rare instance of Bond *not being in control* of the situation in a film--.

Bond hovers over her body as Oddjob and Goldfinger's minions approach to capture him. In any other context or narrative lead-up, Connery's blankness as he kneels beside Tilly's body could be seen as flat, but because there is an appropriate leadup to this moment --screenwriters, producers/directors, and actors working in tandem to reach this--, it gives us an excellent visualization of Bond's internal monologue. As we see Connery we can almost hear Fleming's own words when describing Jill Masterson's death in the original novel: "More death! More blood on his hands…"

By comparison, the way Fleming's Bond deals with Tilly's death is completely inconsistent with how the character has been developed through the course of the six novels that preceded *Goldfinger*; It even contradicts Bond's characterization *inside* the narrative of the same novel.

Instead of the emotional toll and contradiction, Bond's reaction is relegated to one sentence delivered to Felix Leiter --who is assisting Bond in stopping Goldfinger--: "Poor little bitch. She didn't think much of men". The quip references Tilly's lesbianism in the novel, and it is unclear if Bond --or Fleming-- has any contempt for the character because of her homosexuality.

The result, interestingly, comes off as flat as many supposedly emotional moments found throughout the Bond film canon. It is a superb example of how even the original novels suffer when Fleming departs from the original vision of the character of James Bond.

An assumption can be made that this is a showcase of growth on behalf of the character, an instance of Bond being able to detach his feelings from the job at hand in a more effective way; However, there are no moments like this in the novels and short stories that came after *Goldfinger*. As a matter of fact, the emotional state of the character gradually degenerates as the novels go on, with a noticeable dip in Fleming's 1964 novel *You Only Live Twice* --as a product of his wife's death--.

Paradoxically, it is the cinematic interpretation of the scene that delivers a resonance that is absent in the literary original. The screenwriters, the producers/director, and Connery stayed true to Fleming's vision of Bond, even when Fleming himself departed from his idea. The result is a vastly superior and memorable scene.

Unfortunately, beyond these two instances, we never see this level of emotional contradiction and depth for the rest of the Connery outings. It is important to underline yet again that this is no reason to disqualify any of his Bond outings as trite and low-quality; On the contrary, they are classic films whose cultural importance cannot be understated --and this goes for every single Bond adventure in the franchise--. Connery's Bond venerably sparked a massive cultural revolution in the nineteen-sixties and has thrilled and entertained entire generations of people for over fifty years. It is merely when one gets to the details of his tenure that we start seeing the cracks produced by the nature of this adaptation.

Connery's Bond tenure, then, can be surmised as following the Fleming plotlines but detaching Fleming's Bond from the stories. The results are films that succeed in their function as escapist adventures, but that are often devoid of emotional depth and contradiction. It is this exact emphasis on both escapism over a faithful adaptation of the Bond character that would set the stage for the coming, increasingly outlandish Bond adventure.

GEORGE LAZENBY

Much like Timothy Dalton himself, George Lazenby is considered to be an outlier in the Bond film canon. His sole outing, 1969's *On Her Majesty's Secret Service*, received a mixed reception --despite being one of the biggest box office attractions of the year [7] --, with much of the criticism aimed at Lazenby's performance as Bond. Writing for *The Guardian*, Derek Malcolm wrote that Lazenby "is not a good actor and though I never thought Sean Connery was all that stylish either, there are moments when one yearns for a little of his liche panache.[8] ", while other critics like Donald Zec of *The Daily Mirror* were less kind, writing that "[Lazenby] looks uncomfortably in the part like a size four foot in a size ten gumboot [9]."

With a reaction as mixed --and with scathing jabs at Lazenby's performance-- one would not be surprised at the fact that the Bond producers decided to re-stabilize the franchise by bringing Connery back for one last foray as Bond in 1971's *Diamonds Are Forever*. But the reality is that they were intending to continue with Lazenby through-and-through; Even offering him a contract for seven films as James Bond [10]. As it happens, the reason why Lazenby did only one Bond film is because of Lazenby's own decision to not continue with the part.

A startling decision for a person that, with no acting experience, managed to bluff his way into the role of James Bond --making him a world-renowned star for the time--.

Lazenby's gripes with Bond, stardom, and the unique filmmaking process of a Bond film were insurmountable and unlike his way of being. "The producers made me feel like I was mindless," Lazenby said in a 1969 interview, "They disregarded everything I suggested simply because I hadn't been in the film business like them for about a thousand years."[11].

To make matters worse, the cultural context of the late sixties added another layer of distance between Lazenby and the Bond character. In a 2012 interview, Lazenby recounted:

> "People were going to Easy Rider, that was the big movie of the time. There was hardly any young person that didn't have long hair. And you can imagine how I felt walking around with short hair trying to get laid. I looked like a cop or a waiter, and people were about peace and not war, and Bond was all about war [...] I was convinced it was not going to survive." 12

In the end --and much like Timothy Dalton after him-- George Lazenby was not able to prove his worth as a Bond actor. But whereas Dalton did not have the chance to do so, Lazenby took a conscious decision to not continue pursuing the role. What we are left with is a lone, yet highly entertaining and classic Bond adventure, as well as the producer's first attempt --and failure-- to bring

Bond closer to Fleming.

On Her Majesty's Secret Service has the distinction of being --plot-wise-- the most faithful adaptation of any of the original Fleming novels. While a handful of scenes are added, almost every element present in the book makes its way to the cinematic version, the only omissions being continuity issues, such as the mentioning that Bond visits Vesper Lynd's grave every year, and one or two major flips in character motivations. Unfortunately, while entire scenes, conflicts, characters, and interactions manage to appear in the film, we still do not get an accurate and complex portrayal of Fleming's vision of Bond.

This is, however, unsurprising given the context in which *On Her Majesty's Secret Service* was being made. With the Bond franchise already becoming a massive entity in the film industry, it made sense to stick to the established cinematic interpretation of Bond for commercial purposes, as well as ensuring a successful transition out of Connery --given an existing anxiety that audiences would not be able to accept any other actor interpreting the role of James Bond [13]--. So, much like Connery before him, Lazenby's Bond followed the path charted for the cinematic Bond since the inception of the series. The only exception being an added injection of masculinity in order to take advantage of Lazenby's physical capabilities.

As *On Her Majesty's Secret Service*'s director Peter Hunt put it in a 1968 interview:

> *"We wanted someone who oozed sexual assurance, and we think this fellow has that. Just wait until the women see him on screen ... I am not saying he is an actor. There is a great deal of difference between an actor and a film star.*

Didn't they find Gary Cooper when he was an electrician?
14

The overt injection of surplus masculinity into the Bond character makes for added entertainment in the realm of the escapist fantasy that the Bond films typically operate in. However, the producers decided to do so while at the same time sticking close to the plotline of what is --essentially-- one of the most emotional Fleming novels.

The same dissonance that plagued most of the Connery films, that of the character not being in tune with what the story calls for, is present twofold in Lazenby's sole outing as Bond, in turn severely hampering what is a valiant and brave acting effort on Lazenby's part, who before Bond never did any acting whatsoever.

The perceived flatness of Lazenby's performance can be seen once again in how the character projects himself when in situations where --at least theoretically-- all control is taken away from him. At the beginning of the novel, Bond is immediately captured by Marc-Ange Draco's men after successfully saving Teresa (Tracy) from suicide. As he is taken to Draco's office, Bond remains silent, only in possession of a single hidden knife. He remains this way until eventually meeting Draco.

In the film, it is the complete opposite: It takes Draco's men three attempts to finally be able to capture Bond. While he is in transit to Draco's office, Bond makes lighthearted quips while showing a relaxed demeanor, and right before entering his office, Bond manages to best his captors and deliver a considerable and frantically edited beating before finally meeting Draco.

The hyper-masculinization of the character means that there is no circumstance in which Bond is bested both physically and emotionally. The action, then, becomes inconsequential since there is no real sense of danger or suspense at the challenges that Bond faces; In equal measures, the relationships that Bond has with other characters are tinged in a layer of artificiality that while maybe effective in 1969 --the time of the sexual revolution--, does not age gracefully.

It is particularly interesting that "Cubby" Broccoli and Harry Saltzman, the original Bond producers, decided to take this approach to Bond for this specific adaptation, since in Fleming's original novel, Bond is impaired by a deteriorating physical condition and a grave sense of *ennui* as a product of his chase for SPECTRE and Ernst Stavro Blofeld. One of the most interesting aspects of the cinematic adaptation of *On Her Majesty's Secret Service* --and one of the only big changes to the story-- is the reversal of Bond's motivation in chasing Blofeld and any remnants of SPECTRE.

In both the film and the novel, Bond considers resigning from the Secret Service; However, the reason Bond reaches this conclusion is vastly different in both versions. In the novel, Bond and MI6 have been chasing after any leads of Blofeld's whereabouts for well over a year. While M remains highly motivated in the pursuit, Bond falls into an existential and emotional limbo, prompting him to draft a letter of resignation:

> *"That was the gist of what he would dictate to his secretary when he got back to the office the day after tomorrow. And*

if she burst into tears, to hell with her! He meant it. By God he did. He was fed to the teeth with chasing the ghost of Blofeld. And the same went for SPECTRE. The thing had been smashed. Even a man of Blofeld's genius, in the impossible event that he still existed, could never get a machine of that caliber running again."

It is essentially Bond's lack of action and motivation that drives him to this decision, and it remains constant throughout the book; It is aging Bond in a quiet fight to regain any semblance of control of his life. Once Bond decides to marry Tracy, the looming shadow of the resignation letter acquires an added sense of gravitas that adds to the emotional state of Bond --and the eventual shock of Tracy's death--.

In the film, however, it is the inverse: It is Bond who is still highly motivated to pursue Blofeld, while M is the one that lacks the confidence or motivation to do so. As M relieves Bond of his operative duties in the search for Blofeld, Bond decides to have Moneypenny draft his resignation letter.

Bond then retreats to his office where we see props from previous Bond films. --Red Grant's watch from *From Russia With Love,* the breathing apparatus from *Thunderball,* and more--. He then receives a response from M, who grants Bond his wishes. It is then revealed that Moneypenny modified the letter to make it a temporary leave instead of a full-on resignation. Bond, who regrets his impulsivity, thanks Moneypenny for modifying the intention of the letter at the last minute.

The matter of Bond's resignation is introduced and resolved in two scenes, and thus, the film loses an added layer of emotional tension that the source material provides both for Bond and Tracy, which in turn makes a lot of Lazenby's actions as Bond inconsequential, and therefore flat. The *ennui* at his job --as seen at the beginning of the novel-- is the key character element that makes Bond fall in love with Tracy the way he does; Tracy invigorates Bond towards the latter half of the novel because she represents the very humanity and purpose he seeks to regain. However, the wealth of three-dimensional characterization found in Fleming's original novel is unfortunately lost in the path charted for the cinematic version of Bond.

In essence, Lazenby's Bond compounds the detachment to Fleming's original characterization --introduced in the Connery films-- and builds on it thanks to the emphasis on the sexualization and hyper-masculinization of the character. When paired with the faithfulness to the original plot for *On Her Majesty's Secret Service*, the dissonance is evident, and the performance comes off as stilted and distanced.

Bond's relationship with Tracy, the core aspect of the original novel, loses its romantic and tragic veneer in the cinematic adaptation. Fleming creates an incredible context in which two highly resourceful, strong, and deeply troubled characters connect in a way, unlike Bond, has done since Vesper Lynd. Fleming's language and sentence structure remain rapid and concise --much like the thought process of Bond himself--, but the directness creates a romantic contrast between the otherwise brutish Bond and this entirely new type of relationship he is encountering. Moments such as: "They had not wanted to let go of each other's voices, but finally the last goodnight, the last kiss, had been exchanged…" come as an indication of growth and the sense of Bond regaining control of his life, the nature of the prose changing alongside Bond's emotional state.

Fleming lays it bare for the readers close to the end of *On Her Majesty's Secret Service* when Bond finally meets Tracy after his ordeal in Piz Gloria:

> *"Bond reached out and pressed [Tracy's] hand on the wheel. He hated scenes. But it was true what she said. He hadn't thought of her, only of the job. It never crossed his mind that anybody really cared about him. A shake of the head from his friends when he went, a few careful lines in the obituary columns of The Times, a momentary pang in a few girl's hearts. But now, in three day's time, he would no longer be alone. He would be half of two people. There wouldn't only be May [Bond's maid] and Mary Goodnight [Bond's secretary] who would tut-tut over him when he came back from some job as a hospital case. Now, if he got himself killed, there would be Tracy who would at any rate partially die with him."*

Throughout all the Bond novels and short stories written by Fleming, this single paragraph is the only moment where Bond manages to achieve a level of self-awareness and insight that otherwise would be compartmentalized in any other situation. His admission of being overly focused on the job is a crucial breakdown of one of his strident psychological defense mechanisms: the professional detachment. The realization of his loneliness is a direct consequence of his breakdown, but that leads to the acceptance and enthusiasm for marriage with Tracy; After all, he will become "half of two people."

To give a sense of how this supposes a substantial emotional growth for Bond --and how far the eventual death of Tracy would affect him-- we only have to take a look at the final lines of the final Bond novel: 1965's *The Man With The Golden Gun*. In this case, the book ends with a badly wounded Bond and Mary Goodnight --his secretary-- who have become romantically involved, as they share a quiet moment in Jamaica after completing their mission. Fleming's final lines of the book underline the deeper cynicism that Bond falls into after the events of *On Her Majesty's Secret Service*:

> " 'And James, it's not far from the Liguanea Club and you can go there and play bridge, and golf when you get better. There'll be plenty of people for you to talk to. And then of course I can cook and sew buttons on for you and so on.' Of all the doom-fraught graffiti a woman can write on the wall, those are the most insidious, the most deadly. James Bond, in the full possession of his senses, with his eyes wide open, his feet flat on the linoleum floor, stuck his head between the mink-lined jaws of the trap. He said, and meant it, 'Goodnight. You're an angel.' At the same time, he knew, deep down, that love from Mary Goodnight, or from any other woman, was not enough for him. It would be like taking 'a room with a view'. For James Bond the same view would always pall."

Bond is back colder and more cynical than ever, but with a yearning to go back to his previous mental state --the one seen in *On Her Majesty's Secret Service*--. Fleming's description of "the mink-lined jaws of the trap" underlines the new emotional contradiction. This time it is that of a broken man that managed --to some degree-- to recompose himself but will never return to the high point he used to be with Tracy.

While *On Her Majesty's Secret Service*'s script sticks close to the original Fleming plotline, the producer's vision for Lazenby's Bond distanced the character from what is essentially the emotional climax of the book series. The establishment of Lazenby as a hyper-masculine and hyper-sexual interpretation of Bond grinds hard with the weakened and vulnerable Bond of the novel, and creates a wealth of scenes and interactions where Lazenby's performance has no choice but to buckle under the weight of the narrative disparity; As explained in a previous chapter, Lazenby comes short of the emotional mark that the story calls for to be successful.

On a final note, a real tragedy in the cinematic adaptation of the novel, and the decision to create a more in-control Bond, is that it devalues Tracy's contribution to the story.

In the novel, Fleming makes use of Bond's degraded physical state during his ski escape from Blofeld's alpine base in Piz Gloria. The action is peppered with repeated mentions of the stress taken by Bond's body: "Bond got gingerly to his feet, gasping and spitting snow. One of his bindings had opened. His trembling fingers found the forward latch and banged it tight again." … "The sharp Christie reminded him of his legs and ankles" … "Now he was done for! Not even enough strength to get his hands to his ankles!" … "He got to his feet and, rather light-headed […] started on the last mile of finishing schuss across the meadows to the right" and "Bond, a grey-faced, lunging automaton, somehow stayed upright on the two miles of treacherous langlauf down the gentle slope of Samaden." are examples of how as Bond is being chased and shot down the mountain and into the nearest Swiss town, his stamina is rapidly deteriorating and is progressively losing any control he may have gathered at the beginning of his escape.

When his body cannot take it anymore, and surrender seems to be the only option, Tracy comes in to save the day. Then in one sentence Fleming gives Bond a level of vulnerability seen only before in *Casino Royale* and in *Live and Let Die*'s broken finger:

> " 'Tracy', said Bond dully. 'Tracy. Hold on to me. I'm in bad shape. Tell you later.' "

Tracy then takes control of the situation and aids Bond in his escape from Blofeld's minions. Her sense of cool under pressure and her abilities behind the wheel of her car provides a perfect balance to the similar characteristics of the Bond character: Bond finally finds his equal:

> *"There was something new in the girl's voice, a lilt and happiness that had not been there at Royale. Bond turned and looked at her carefully for the first time. Yes, she was somehow a new woman, radiating health and a kind of inner glow. The tumbled hair glittered with vitality and the half-opened, beautiful lips seemed always to be on the verge of a smile."*

The touching, romantic descriptions on behalf of Fleming are almost entirely new in the lexicon of the novels. The typical sensual descriptions of the Bond women are interwoven with the added softness and poetics of a Bond that is not only in love but finally regaining his sense of humanity.

Unfortunately, while Lazenby briefly exhibits a sense of exhaustion after the ski chase, and we do see Diana Rigg's Tracy showcase a level of proactiveness, the figure of Bond never goes to the depths of vulnerability that the literary version arrives at. The novel utilizes the action of the chase to tell the story of Bond's fragility, his passing of control to Tracy, and their eventual closeness; The film uses the scene as an exciting action set piece and nothing more. Lazenby's Bond eventual proposal to Tracy comes slightly off, since by this point Tracy has disappeared from the narrative for half the film, and Bond has exercised his virile sexuality on two of Blofeld's "Angels of Death". Once again, the contextual influence of the sexual revolution may have played a part in the direction taken --as well as the admitted sexualized direction director Peter Hunt decided to take--, but either way, the disparity between plot and character fails to deliver the full emotional payoff that the scene is supposed to give.

George Lazenby will forever be a controversial and divisive Bond. Part of the reason for it being starring in a singular film in the franchise, the other being the perceived stiltedness of his performance. While putting forth an effort admirable for a first-time actor, Lazenby's Bond is crippled by the filmmaker's decision to continue the line established by Connery's Bond; That of crafting a Bond differentiated from Fleming's original vision while flying close to the original plotlines --which necessitate the reciprocity of the characterization to be effective in their delivery-- and injecting traditionally non-Bond elements such as hyper-masculinity.

While these elements make for an action-packed entry in the series, it further detaches Bond from any emotional depth. This trend would continue to escalate and reach parodical heights in the Bond era that came afterward.

ROGER MOORE

By the time Roger Moore was slated to become the latest actor to play the role of Bond, the producers were weighed down by two great anxieties.

The first was the ongoing fear that the general audience would not accept any actor other than Sean Connery playing the role. A persistent and rational fear, considering that the franchise was coming off an outing with George Lazenby that, despite being a commercial success, grossed half of the total worldwide box-office gross of the previous Bond adventure --1967's *You Only Live Twice* starring Connery as Bond-- [15]. To further compound these fears, Connery's eventual final film in the role, 1971's *Diamonds Are Forever*, was a considerable commercial success that managed to easily beat *On Her Majesty's Secret Service*'s worldwide box-office tally --$64.6 million [16] versus $116 million[17]--.

The second anxiety resided in Moore himself, who by that point was a recognizable figure in television; Having starred as Simon Templar in Leslie Charteris' classic series *The Saint*, and as

Lord Brett Sinclair --alongside Tony Curtis-- in Robert S. Baker's *The Persuaders!*

The producers were concerned about Moore's potential typecasting in said roles, preventing audiences from accepting him as James Bond [18]. So to answer these two dilemmas, the filmmakers decided to distance themselves from Connery's Bond portrayal, and instead, mold the character to suit Moore's persona. To quote Moore himself:

> *"I suppose because I was more relaxed I really could make James Bond Roger Moore rather than Roger Moore James Bond."* 19

The result was a direct opposite to Connery in every aspect possible. The Bond films became more lighthearted and comedic in tone, as opposed to the more serious Connery adventures. The need to separate Moore from Connery became such a main characteristic of this portrayal of the character, that Bond stopped smoking cigarettes, stopped ordering Martinis, and even stopped driving Aston Martins; Instead, Moore's Bond substituted them by smoking cigars, favoring Bourbon, and driving Lotuses.

The result helped transcend the Bond film franchise from a cultural fad of the sixties to a full-on cinematic institution; With films like 1977's *The Spy Who Loved Me* and *1979*'s *Moonraker* becoming massive successes even surpassing the original Connery films --with *Moonraker* becoming the highest-grossing Bond film until *1995*'s *Goldeneye*--.

Perhaps more notably, Moore's Bond managed to beat Connery's unofficial return to the Bond role at the box-office, with

1983's *Octopussy* grossing $180 million [20] over the $160 million [21] grossed by the non-EON productions Bond film *Never Say Never Again*, proving once and for all that the character of James Bond is bigger than the actor that portrays him.

However, with this further removal from Connery's portrayal, comes an increased removal from the original vision of the character of James Bond.

It comes as no surprise that more contemporary perceptions of Moore's Bond have increasingly fallen out of favor with modern audiences --mainly thanks to an increased appreciation for a more Fleming-centric Bond-- [22]. The added side-effect of the decision to further remove Bond from Fleming's vision, and the added emphasis on the action/adventure fantasy, made for moments that are not exactly fondly remembered by fans and general audiences alike.

Scenes like the gondola chase from 1979's *Moonraker*, where Bond utilizes a hovercraft gondola to cross Saint Mark's square in Venice --complete with a pigeon performing a double-take--, or Bond performing a Tarzan yell while jumping through vines in 1983's *Octopussy* signified moments where the Bond franchise became self-parodical at best, and pastiche at worst. While incredibly popular for its time, the results became dated even by standards of the nineteen-eighties, when action films became increasingly more gritty and violent.

Perhaps the most striking aspect of the producer's departure from Connery's Bond --and by consequence Fleming's-- is how clear it becomes that they struggled to find a direction in which to take Roger Moore's James Bond. His first two films, 1973's *Live and*

Let Die and 1974's *The Man With The Golden Gun* are perhaps some of the most experimental films in the Bond canon; With the filmmakers testing the waters into the many directions Bond could be taken.

For *Live And Let Die*, the humor and light-heartedness are immediately established, but they are noticeably toned down when compared to the rest of the Moore films. As a result, there is a tonal inconsistency between Moore's demeanor and the otherwise serious and supernatural tone of the film. A great example of this tonal inconsistency can be found in a scene where Moore's Bond threatens Rosie Carver with a gun over her perceived betrayal. Moore alternates between the serious and aggressive nature of a Bond reminiscent of Sean Connery and the relaxed, seductive, and debonair flair that comes naturally to him. The result is a dissonant and weirdly out-of-character portrayal of Bond, where he does not seem to showcase either assertiveness or understanding.

A similar scene occurs in *The Man With The Golden Gun*, where Bond becomes more aggressive with Andrea Andres -- Scaramanga's mistress-- to the point of becoming physical with her. This is one of the only instances where the filmmakers tried bringing Moore closer to Connery's portrayal of Bond, but Moore's physicality is way too relaxed and debonair and does not sell a performance that calls for Connery's brutish assertiveness --as a matter of fact, Moore's Bond would not be this aggressive to a female counterpart for the rest of his tenure in the character--.

Another instance of experimentation is how both films utilize a cinematic fad of the time as a crutch on which to rest the film on. *Live and Let Die* utilizes the genre trappings of Blaxploitation --a short-lived yet popular subgenre that emerged from the early seventies, and that dealt with stories of African American social realities and fantasies-- to wrap its story around, while *The Man With The Golden Gun* deals with the then-popular Kung-Fu sub-genre that films like 1973's *Enter The Dragon* helped popularize.

Except for 1979's *Moonraker* --which tapped into Star Wars-mania--, this decision was in no doubt born out of the aforementioned anxiety the producers had of a new and different Bond. By leaning on established genres, they were ensuring themselves that they had a pre-built audience in the case that the general public rejected Roger Moore as James Bond.

These are merely some of the biggest examples of this directorial uncertainty at the beginning of the Moore era, but the makeup of the remaining films point to this uncertainty not going away since after the success of 1977's *The Spy Who Loved Me*, all the remaining Moore films followed the same formula as the 1977 film.

This is not to say that previous Bond adventures did not follow a certain predetermined pattern, but they were infinitely more playful in their presentation --ironically a byproduct of sticking close to Fleming's plotlines--.

1965's *Thunderball* starts the story at a health clinic, much like the original novel. 1967's *You Only Live Twice* plays around with the perceived death of James Bond. 1971's *Diamonds Are Forever*'s debrief with M is unique in its visual explanation of the key aspects of diamond smuggling. Comparing this to the matter-of-factness of Moore's Bond hitting the necessary beats in the similar fashion --debriefing with M, flirting with Moneypenny, a visit to Q branch and off to the mission-- helps create the sense that while at the beginning of Moore's tenure the producers were seemingly throwing everything at the wall to see what stuck, by the end they were playing it safe.

Even so, all the Bond films follow some sort of formula that they all play around with either in presentation or timing in the narrative, this is nowhere to be found in the later Bond films starring Moore.

Perhaps the only instance where the producers made a conscious decision to bring Moore slightly closer to Fleming's Bond was in 1981's *For Your Eyes Only*. Following the outlandishness of 1979's *Moonraker*, there came a necessity to return Bond to a more serious and down-to-earth outing [23]. The result was *For Your Eyes Only*, the one Moore Bond film distinct for being the one closest to the original Fleming source material.

Portraying more realistic villains, characters, and increasing the violence definitively brings a much necessary balance to Moore's humor and light-heartedness, but here we are faced with the same issue that plagued Connery's and Lazenby's Bond: The story is decidedly Fleming-esque, but the direction taken for Bond does not merge well with what the story calls for. In the same way that Moore looks uncomfortable being aggressive and assertive with female characters in his first two Bond films, Moore does not necessarily look at ease in the otherwise darker elements of the plot. This discomfort becomes evident in many scenes with Melina Havelock, who is on a path of revenge against the people that murdered her parents.

While herself not an adaptation of Fleming's original character --*Judy* Havelock--, the nature of her character is decidedly reminiscent of Fleming: A strong, mysterious and beautiful female character that while showcasing determination, possesses an inner emotional conflict --much like Bond himself--.

Melina possesses these traits reminiscent of a Fleming character, but Moore, by a combination of character direction and performance, seems too fatherly and too seemingly disgusted at the darkness within Melina. This adds to another inconsistency in the characterization of Bond since Moore *does* explore a similar dark depth in the same film. The scene in question may be the moment where Roger Moore's Bond comes closest to Fleming's original vision of the character: The killing of Emile Locque.

Locque, an assassin, runs Countess Lisl Von Schlaf over with a beach buggy, killing her in front of Bond. Moore's reaction, while still exceedingly contained, manages to convey an inkling of an interior monologue similar to that of Fleming's Bond when reacting to Jill Masterson's death in the *Goldfinger* novel: "More blood! More death…"

What follows is a private and personal vow of revenge that Moore's Bond does not share with anyone, and keeps to himself. Another moment where Moore comes close to the internalization of Fleming's original characterization. Later in the film, Bond manages to best Locque, who lies injured --thanks to a bullet fired by Bond-- in a car on the verge of falling from an Albanian cliff. Bond approaches the car, and after a brief exchange, kicks it, causing it to finally fall; Killing Locque before any request for mercy is heard.

This unusually cold moment for Moore brings him fairly close to what the script calls for Bond to do both tonally and thematically for the rest of the film, and in the process, brings him closer to Fleming's vision of the character. The consequential nature of the Countesses' death --even though Moore does not display much beyond a quip-- is made evident in the way Bond handles the death of Locque. The contradiction of the situation also highlights the moral and emotional throughline of the Fleming novels but on a smaller scale: Locque, the silent and brutal killer, is at the verge of begging for mercy, while Moore's Bond, who is almost always presented as relaxed and charismatic, remains silent and cold-blooded at the action to come.

While brilliant and an iconic scene in its own right, it remains however a fleeting one. The one-liner delivered by Bond afterward effectively bookends this otherwise anomalous moment for Moore: "He had no head for heights."

The inherent moral grittiness and darkness of Fleming's Bond do not mean that the novels --and the character-- are devoid of any humor whatsoever. Fleming adds these instances in very subtle and concise ways throughout many of the novels. An instance can be found in his 1955 novel *Moonraker*, when Bond and Gala Brand --the Bond girl-- decide to swim at a beach without their clothes on. Gala is shy at the prospect of undressing herself in front of Bond:

> " 'We shall be perfectly respectable and there's no one to see me, and I promise not to look,' he lied cheerfully, leading the way round the next bend in the cliff."

The humor in the novels is almost always present in relation to Bond and the Bond girl, or with the very few people he can call his "friends" --Mathis, Felix Leiter, Quarrel--. While the humor with the female characters is playful, flirty, and sensual in many instances, the humor with characters like Mathis or Felix Leiter is more ironic and sarcastic. Mathis' reaction to Bond's monologue on the nature of evil in *Casino Royale* is a great example:

> " 'Bravo,' said Mathis. 'I'm proud of you. You ought to be tortured every day. I really must remember to do something evil this evening. I must start at once. I have a few marks in my favour -- only small ones, alas,' he added ruefully -- 'but I shall work fast now that I have seen the light. What a splendid time I'm going to have. Now let's see, where shall we start, murder, arson, rape? But no, these are peccadilloes. I must really consult the good Marquis de Sade. I am a child, an absolute child in these matters.”

Fleming uses light-hearted or humoristic elements to bring characters together in the narrative and to provide a counterpoint and a balance to the dark nature of James Bond's world. The humor, however, never takes center stage to the point where it overtakes the thematic elements of the story or even the action at hand. This is something that has remained fairly consistent throughout all the different portrayals of the character of Bond, but with Moore it overtakes the vast majority of the on-screen action.

The aforementioned examples of the Tarzan yell and the gondola chase in Venice are merely two instances of the comedic element divorcing Bond from the narrative. Henchmen like Jaws falling in love in 1979's *Moonraker*, Snowboarding to the tune of the Beach Boys in 1985's *A View to a Kill*, and Bond accidentally swallowing a golden bullet in 1974's *The Man With The Golden Gun* are more examples of the humor taking center stages in the on-screen action that, while entertaining to watch, does not serve the story and the characters in any way other than the entertainment value.

Along with the excess humor also comes excess in the fantasy elements of the Bond stories.

While riveting in its own right, the dependency on ever-increasingly ridiculous and intentionally comedic gadgets stretches the audience's suspension of disbelief to insurmountable lengths. Before long, Moore's Bond began using crocodile submersibles, a Lotus Esprit submarine, a boat disguised as an iceberg, and the infamous gondola hovercraft.

While the gadgetry is one of the key elements of the cinematic version of James Bond, with Moore it is taken to extreme lengths; At worst, they look like parodies of the actual gadgets James Bond would use --Pierce Brosnan's Bond would face similar scrutiny with the invisible Aston Martin from 2002's *Die Another Day*--.

Along with this necessity to keep pushing Bond into being bigger than ever before, comes increasingly fantastical plots; The most notable example being Bond's venture into outer space in 1979's *Moonraker*, a plot decision that while popular for the time, is constantly cited as being one of the reasons why *Moonraker* is considered to be the worst film of the franchise [24][25][26]. This three-fold stress on the audience's suspension of disbelief, the over-emphasized humor, the over-exaggerated gadgetry, and the fantastical plots make for films that do not necessarily stand the test of time and have become divisive within the Bond film canon.

This is not to say, however, that Fleming did not have a penchant for the excess. His 1958 novel *Dr. No* is a perfect example where --for a singular time--, Bond became more Spy-fi than adventure espionage, with the most notable scene of the book being Bond's battle with a giant squid as he escapes Dr. No's torture maze.

However, the outlandishness of the setup is grounded by an extra dose of grit in different places. Honey Rider --the female counterpart for Bond-- recounts a chilling story of sexual abuse and her eventual diabolical revenge. Fleming paints an image of Jamaica in the process of decay [27], and the various deaths in the novel are described in unusually violent detail. The result of the balance, as well as the nature of Fleming's writing, still makes for a suspenseful and grounded journey for Bond and the audience regardless of the fantastical elements; That balance is absent for the always-in-control and always relaxed Roger Moore.

The threefold pushing of the audience's suspension of disbelief ends up inevitably divorcing Moore's Bond from any emotional consequentiality, and the audience's original perception of James Bond as a character as well.

However, it needs to be said that these elements are exactly what elevated the franchise from a fad of the sixties to a full-fledged cinematic institution. In making Bond larger-than-life, the filmmakers allowed for the character to break the confinement of the cinema screen, managing to secure his place in the collective consciousness for generations to come, and this is an achievement that not only can be attributed to the filmmakers, but to Roger Moore himself. It is only a shame that what the audience saw was more Roger Moore than James Bond.

PIERCE BROSNAN

With Pierce Brosnan, the new producers of the Bond film franchise --Barbara Broccoli and Michael G. Wilson-- managed to transform James Bond from a cultural staple of the twentieth century to a hero of the new Millenium.

By modernizing Bond's relationship with the world around him --and its new threats--, they managed to preserve a certain integrity to the character, while at the same time injecting a new-found relevance and importance to his role as Secret Agent. In 1995's *Goldeneye*, Bond is faced with remnants of Cold War mentality turned dangerous --including himself--, in 1997's *Tomorrow Never Dies*, Bond comes face to face with the new destructive power of information, in 1999's *The World is Not Enough*, Bond confronts the changing face of terrorism --a vicious change from the SPECTRE days--, and in 2002's *Die Another Day*, the real-life tensions between North and South Korea are explored. While the films preserve a flippant sense of fantasy, much of the plots are still rooted in contexts that expand beyond the Cold War framework of East versus West.

A lot of what made this transitioning phase smoother was

Pierce Brosnan himself, who carries an enviable effortlessness in playing Bond. He looks at ease and fitting in a Casino, underneath the sheets, and in the middle of any fist-fight or shootout; His performance became an instant hit with audiences and critics alike, a reaction reflected in the commercial success of his four films, with *Goldeneye, The World is Not Enough* and *Die Another Day* becoming the highest-grossing Bond films at their respective time of release [28] [29].

It can be argued that the reason for Brosnan's success as Bond is two-fold. First and foremost, it's Brosnan's demeanor and physicality --as previously mentioned--. The second is the decision to bring up a more balanced approach to the James Bond character. With the notable exception of 1995's *Goldeneye*, Brosnan's Bond exhibits all the requisite traits that the cinematic version of the character possesses --coolness under pressure, humor, British gentlemanship, snobbiness, seductiveness, and danger--, but never utilizes any of these traits as a central pillar in which to base the performance around.

Brosnan's Bond does not have the animalistic physicality of Sean Connery nor the hyper-masculinity of Lazenby, but at the same time, he does not exhibit the debonair ease of Roger Moore. The result is a one-size-fits-all type of Bond, one that can easily fit into the incredibly different context the franchise had to operate in the nineties, and a Bond that benefited primarily from the inherent aesthetics of Pierce Brosnan as an actor.

The downside to this approach, however, is that it tends to devoid Bond of a lot of emotional contradiction and depth, and oftentimes makes him and the rest of the characters subservient to the plot of the film. In the best of situations, the plot itself becomes a mechanism to question and contradict the nature of James Bond --and other characters-- as is the case in *Goldeneye*, but in the worst cases, Bond becomes an automaton designed to hit the next narrative beat, as is the case of *Die Another Day*.

While previous Bond films were hindered by certain directions that were taken for the Bond character, Brosnan's Bond films are hindered by the conscious decision to *not* take a particular definite direction.

This exact lack of direction clashes harshly with the attempts to draw any emotional element out of the characters and plotlines of the majority of Brosnan's Bond films. A clear example of this can be found in 1997's *Tomorrow Never Dies*, more specifically, in Bond's relationship with Paris Carver.

What would have the potentiality of a Fleming set up -- an old flame of Bond coming center-stage into the mission, her demise and what would be the eventual emotional reckoning with Bond-- is treated as a passing sub-plot, with its emotional resonance being introduced and wrapped up by the end of what is essentially the second act of the film. It seems that its purpose is to introduce a personal edge between Bond and Elliot Carver --the villain--, but the personal revenge aspect is limited to one of Carver's minions and executor of Paris: Dr. Kauffman. It would come as no surprise that by the end of the film one would have forgotten that this even happened in the first place.

Besides the eventual handling of Bond's reaction to Paris' demise at the hands of Carver, the very same scenes between Bond and Paris are handled with a soap-opera level of superficiality -- complete with a very public slap on Bond's face by Paris-- that further fails to engage the audience in what would be the emotional hook of the story. Perhaps a key reason why there was a hesitation to go further with Bond in this arena, and therefore exploring the darkness of the character, stems from the perceived failures of Brosnan's predecessor in tackling these issues.

1999's *The World is Not Enough* does make a better attempt to include some emotional resonance and contradiction into the character of the film. The premise of it is an impressively modernized version of another Fleming-esque setup: Bond falls in love with Elektra King, heiress of oil tycoon Sir Robert King, after playing a key role in the assassination of her father. King is then revealed to be the mastermind behind her ex-captor Renard, and the intellectual executor of her father's assassination. The Fleming elements of Bond's sense of duty versus his emotions are present, along with the updated modern context and threats in the shapelessness of Renard's terrorist cell, and an interesting twist in making the subject of Bond's affection the villainous mastermind in the film. It goes in line with one of Fleming's key philosophies when writing Bond novels:

> *"This so-called hero of mine has a good time. He beats the villain in the end and gets the girl and he even serves his government well. But in the process of that he's got to suffer something in return for his success. I mean, what do you do, dock him something on his income tax? I really tire of the fact that the hero in other people's thrillers gets a bang on the head with a revolver butt and he's perfectly happy afterwards--just a bump on his head."* 30

This writing philosophy reaches its maximum expression with the betrayal and suicide of Vesper Lynd in *Casino Royale*, as well as Tracy's murder in *On Her Majesty's Secret Service*, but it takes other shapes and forms as well. It can be physical punishment like Bond's broken finger in *Live and Let Die*, or the beating given to him by the Spang gang in *Diamonds Are Forever*; And it can also be emotional or mental, as in his amnesia at the end of *You Only Live Twice*, or the acknowledgment of the futility of his affair with Mary Goodnight in *The Man With The Golden Gun*. Fleming's drive to gradually chip away at Bond, and his eventual success -- or failure-- to overcome these physical and emotional hurdles is what deepens and expands his character in ways that do not limit him as a simple spy or action hero.

So in *The World is Not Enough*, the filmmakers had the elements that could make for a Fleming set up with a twist: Bond once again opening himself up emotionally to a woman, who then turns out to be the villain, and eventually, it is up to Bond to take her out --further underlining the tension between his sense of duty and his emotions--. Unfortunately, because of the balanced portrayal that was pursued for Brosnan, this setup is completely stilted in execution; Not because of reasons similar to *Tomorrow Never Dies*' handling of Paris' and Bond's relationship, but because of the introduction of Dr. Christmas Jones.

Denise Richards' portrayal as nuclear physicist Dr. Christmas Jones remains --to this day-- the biggest blemish in the film. Not only because of the sub-par acting on behalf of Richards, but because of the impact, her character has on the narrative. While Sophie Marceau's Elektra King is introduced early in the narrative and is progressively fleshed out throughout --including her relationship with Bond--, Dr. Jones is introduced halfway through the film, and the depth of her character is limited to plot exposition, and to provide Bond with a new love interest.

It is this last element that interferes with the potential emotional depth that the King/Bond subplot could provide. The existence of Dr. Jones softens any emotional blow that may have been dealt with by the outcome of Bond's relationship with King, since once she is killed by him, Bond just switches his attention and affection to Dr. Jones. It renders the scene of Elektra's death emotionally inconsequential for Bond; Any exploration of contradiction and tension from within the character is immediately thrown out the window since Bond now has Dr. Jones to fall back on.

In sticking close to the spirit of the Fleming originals, the filmmakers craft the possibility for a more emotionally complex and compelling Bond film, one that would also take full advantage of Pierce Brosnan's full range as a Bond actor. But in the absence of a specific direction in which to take Brosnan's Bond, the setup does not reach its fullest potential thanks to Dr. Jones, whose presence in the film is merely for commercial purposes.

The casting of Denise Richards --a popular actress among young adults at the time-- is a clear indication of this, as well as the producers signing a marketing partnership with MTV, where over one-hundred hours of Bond-related programming were aired at the time of the film's release --all them hosted by Denise Richards herself-- [31].

This trend of Brosnan as a balanced Bond reaches its most absurd heights in 2002's *Die Another Day*. A movie that while highly entertaining, is a complete triumph of plot over character; And one that once again, places Bond dangerously close in the realm of self-parody seen before in Moore's tenure as Bond -- although even Roger Moore had a negative reaction to the film: "I just thought it went too far - and that's from me, the first Bond in space! Invisible cars and dodgy CGI footage? Please!" [32]--. *Die Another Day* is probably the maximum exponent of the cinematic version of Bond, one that is completely divorced from its literary roots and the key characteristics of Fleming's vision, and that repeatedly quotes and references the key elements that were introduced in the films --ones that became iconic in their own right--.

This vision of Bond is more akin to suave super-hero, a far cry from the flawed and brutalist anti-hero of the source material. The result is a further removal of any depth of character than ever seen before; And while many setpieces remain great to this day, it is not enough to sustain an effective and impactful story, especially when considering the gratuitous amount of computer-generated images, and setups that defy any semblance of suspension of disbelief --like the scene where Bond kite-surfs a tsunami--.

However, while the majority of Brosnan's Bond films consistently display the consequences of a clear lack of direction, 1995's *Goldeneye* proves to be the biggest outlier in his tenure.

Unlike its successors, *Goldeneye* has a clear and definite idea of where to take the character of James Bond. This direction stems from a key question that pervaded general audiences in the early-nineties: Is James Bond relevant in a post-Cold War world? Of course, the filmmakers answer the question with a resounding "Yes", but they do so by maximizing story, characters, acting, cinematography, direction, and music towards this goal.

In *Goldeneye*, James Bond is presented as a walking anachronism, a character who on paper seems without a war or enemies to fight, but in practice, becomes better suited for the emerging challenges that come with a shifting political context. The portrayal of Bond's world receives the same treatment: While previous cinematic adventures boasted colorful and beautifully saturated and clear cinematography, *Goldeneye* consistently shrouds its world and characters in fog and darkness, and favoring muted colors along with higher-contrast low-key lighting; A reflection of the sinister characters that move in and out of shadows with ease --including Bond--.

This invasive sense of darkness is also present in the musical score by French composer Eric Serra. For the most part, the brassy and sexy orchestrations of previous Bond films disappear in favor of a more percussion-heavy electronic soundtrack. Russian choirs ominously chant alongside dark and gloomy electronic drones, while motifs from the James Bond theme are either underplayed or are heavily distorted thanks to a synthesized sound. The result does not create the usual dose of Bond escapism, but instead, it creates an ominous and sinister environment, where allegiances shift easily and perceived friends turn into enemies.

These audiovisual elements converge on the thematic nature of the story: Alec Trevelyan, once Bond's 00-agent counterpart at MI6, is now head of an emerging stateless terrorist organization: the aptly named "Janus" syndicate. The Janus moniker referencing the two-faced Roman God, an element that is also visually reflected on the natures of both Bond and Trevelyan.

The Bond / Trevelyan duality harkens back to the moral throughline that Fleming established for his novels in *Casino*

Royale, the one where history moves so fast that heroes and villains change parts all the time. Trevelyan is what Bond could have become after the end of the Cold War, and Bond is what Trevelyan could have been had he stayed in the MI6.

The script never treats one as superior to the other, instead showcasing them to be in constant competition: sometimes Bond gets the upper hand, but most times Trevelyan comes out on top. Bond meets his match not so much because of the villain being immensely wealthy, megalomaniac, or well-established and powerful, and more so because Trevelyan acts as a shadow self to Bond; Constantly challenging his continuous role as Secret Agent.

The challenges to Bond's relevance and existence also carry over to the female characters in the film. Whereas in previous films Bond would liberally flirt with Moneypenny, in *Goldeneye* she is fairly quick to remark to Bond that: "This sort of behavior could qualify as sexual harassment." A nod to the changing gender roles and politically correct nature of the nineties. M --now played by Dame Judi Dench-- delivers a more scathing and direct commentary on Bond's nature: "I think you're a sexist, misogynist dinosaur. A relic of the Cold War." An overt delineating of the dilemma posed by the film.

However, as far as female characters are concerned, Natalya Simonova carries the most sustained and subtle challenge to Bond's persona. Natalya carries the distinction of being one of the first Bond girls to possess a skill that Bond does not have, and is of paramount importance to the overall narrative: computer hacking.

This decision equals Natalya to Bond himself, and her importance in the narrative--and her emotional arc-- elevates her beyond the archetype of the love conquest. The filmmakers even play this now-equalized relationship for effective laughs at several points in the film, where after receiving a severe command from Natalya, an astonished Bond replies by saying: "Yes, sir." While this type of relationship is unique to the Bond film franchise, it is more commonplace in the Fleming novels.

The closest proxy to the Bond / Natalya relationship is without a doubt Bond's relationship to Gala Brand in Fleming's 1955 novel *Moonraker*. In the same way that Natalya possesses the necessary computing skills to disrupt and sabotage the GoldenEye satellite, Gala Brand possesses the skills to safeguard the Moonraker ballistic missile. Both Bonds necessitate to gain their trust, and eventually, ensure that they use their skillset to save the world.

Natalya also directly confronts Bond about the dual nature and moral relativism of his work as Secret Agent; Calling into question his seeming comfort in deciding that his friend must be killed --once again calling back to Bond's ability to compartmentalize his feelings in the novels--. And in an expertly delivered and surprisingly Dalton-esque manner, Bond coldly replies: "It's what keeps me alive."

Connecting all these elements is Brosnan's portrayal of Bond, which is more somber and aggressive when compared to his successive adventures.

The irony and specific brand of humor characteristic of Brosnan are still there, but *Goldeneye*'s Bond is more prone to bouts of aggression --as seen in the Janus train stand-off--, as well as quiet moments of introspection --such as in his confrontational conversation with Natalya in Cuba--. It is the closest Brosnan's Bond ever comes to the consequential range of emotions as seen in Fleming's Bond, and it creates a compelling interplay between the villains and the secondary characters in the film.

The James Bond seen in *Goldeneye* is not always in control of the situation, his tension between emotion versus the sense of duty is present, and now not only does he face a highly personal and highly skilled threat, but his relevance is being questioned on a metaphysical level.

When put in context with the other three Brosnan Bond adventures, *Goldeneye* stands out almost as an anomaly. Not only is it the most stylized film in his tenure, but it also contains a Bond character that is not quite what the audiences would eventually get accustomed to as time went on.

Brosnan's Bond is mostly associated with his irresistible flair and charm, as well as hyper-kinetic action setpieces, outlandish gadgets, and one-liners. One would assume that *Goldeneye* was written for a different actor in mind, and these assumptions would be correct: by the time screenwriter Michael France had completed his original draft for the script, Dalton was still slated to return as Bond. [33]

Regardless of this, Pierce Brosnan's tenure and portrayal of Bond remains incredibly popular amongst contemporary audiences; But beyond his popularity, Brosnan's Bond saved the Bond film franchise from irrelevancy, introduced the character to a whole new generation of fans, and helped carry the life and legacy of Ian Fleming well into the new millennium. For these reasons alone, it would not be outrageous to consider Brosnan as possibly the most important Bond actor in the franchise's history.

Brosnan's Bond delivered some of the most memorable moments of the franchise, but unfortunately, a lot of the most embarrassing and ill-remembered moments as well; Something that not only severely handicapped the potential for more emotionally resonating narratives in his time, but also hampers his legacy and longevity for future audiences.

DANIEL CRAIG

The arrival of Daniel Craig into the Bond role signified a complete shake-up of the Bond film canon.

The increasingly fantastical elements of the latter Brosnan Bond films fell out of favor, and producers Barbara Broccoli and Michael G. Wilson decided to take a more serious perspective on Bond; Effectively following a post-911 cultural trend, where there was an increase in demand for highly realistic, violent and gritty action films and television shows, with 2002's *The Bourne Identity* and 2001's *24* becoming only two examples of big hits at the box office and in TV ratings respectively. Along with the decision to restructure the franchise, came the end of a decades-long battle in 1999 to secure the rights of the original Bond novel: *Casino Royale* [34], which was --at the time-- the only novel to not have been adapted into an official EON-produced Bond film.

With all of these ingredients combined, the Bond producers decided to reboot the franchise, and explore the character of Bond from the very beginning of his career as Secret Agent --coincidentally, a decision previously considered by producer "Cubby" Broccoli back in 1986 when Timothy Dalton was cast as Bond[35]--.

This decision was widely regarded as a considerable gamble, and one made riskier with the casting of Daniel Craig as James Bond, which was largely seen by critics and audiences as a massive mistake because of his blonde and blue-eyed look, as well as his short stature [36] [37].

However, five films later, Daniel Craig has quickly become an all-time favorite among critics and audiences alike. Craig's rugged and seemingly more "human" portrayal of Bond became an instant hit amongst new and long-time Bond fans, with films like 2006's *Casino Royale* and 2012's *Skyfall* becoming massive box-office behemoths as a consequence, shattering existing franchise records --as well as overall box-office industry records-- [38].

A big factor in the success is the return to Fleming; Once tried with Dalton, and now rendered more reasonable given the cultural shift in media from the eighties to the early-noughts. The ability to finally adapt *Casino Royale* --easily the most emotionally complex of the Fleming novels-- was in no doubt instrumental to the success and acceptance of Craig as Bond.

Once again, we see Bond not being in total control of any given situation, having to rely on his wit or his sheer brute force to get the upper hand over an opponent. At the same time, we see the depth of emotion that was seemingly absent for a vast portion of the Bond films. All of this is carried effortlessly by Craig, who consistently manages to deliver --at least for the most part-- the challenging internal monologue of the character with effective panache. Behind his cold blue eyes, the audience can get a glimpse of the machinations that both drive Bond and constantly tax him.

In going back to the Fleming source material, Craig's Bond effectively becomes the most direct point of comparison to Timothy Dalton's Bond. Both actors portray the character with the necessary nuance to create a faithful Fleming adaptation, and therefore, a more emotionally resonant version of the character.

However, in stark contrast to Dalton --and oddly enough, the rest of the Bond actors--, the direction the filmmakers took for Craig's Bond in the films following *Casino Royale* --2008's *Quantum of Solace,* 2012's *Skyfall,* and 2015's *Spectre*-- indicate a massive departure from the "back to the roots" model followed so successfully for *Casino Royale* and the Dalton films.

The biggest issue with Craig's Bond is diametrically opposite to that of previous Bond incarnations. While previous Bonds miss the necessary emotional mark for the character, Craig's Bond completely overshoots it, exhibiting an overly-emotional and --in the worst cases-- excessively psychoanalytical version of the character; Once again robbing the audience of the consequentiality of action and emotion that make Bond a compelling character.

It should be noted from the get-go that a lot of this perceived narrative consequentiality in Craig's Bond is --for the most part-- temporary. Meaning that while it may carry an impact from scene to scene, it does not sustain itself throughout the narrative. Once again, the example of Bond's broken finger in Fleming's 1954 novel *Live And Let Die* comes to mind: By choosing to have Bond hampered by this injury, not only does Fleming create a threatening and suspenseful aura around Mr. Big, but it handicaps Bond enough to create the necessary tension to thrill and engage the reader. The consequence of this action is effectively sustained throughout the narrative, and the reader not only undergoes a more suspenseful journey with Bond, but they also learn more about him by the way he nurses --both physically and mentally-- the injury.

Compare this to Bond's gun-shot injury in 2012's *Skyfall*. Throughout the first act of the film, said injury, as well as the effects of Bond's "retirement", are overtly played between characters; So much so that it becomes the very nature of almost every interaction: Mallory berates M for relying on Bond --something he sees as a liability--, Moneypenny jokes with Bond about her shooting him, and Tanner and M are rooting for Bond's recovery on the sidelines. The filmmakers even showcase the perceived effects of this injury visually, by having Bond perform poorly at a marksmanship test --immediately planting the idea that he will not be as skilled with his gun--. However, once the film moves on to Shanghai, it completely throws this set-up away. Except for the shooting of Severine, there is no consistent ramping of the narrative stakes, nor a real sense that Bond is truly and dangerously out of shape. The idea and impact of Bond's injury and "retirement" may have had a consequential impact on a scene-to-scene basis, but it has no emotional resonance for the rest of the narrative.

Comparing such instances in *Skyfall* to similar situations in *Casino Royale* showcases how much the filmmakers had Craig depart from the Fleming formula. Throughout *Casino Royale*, we see Bond make mistakes that have an impact throughout the entire film. This is introduced in the brilliant opening Madagascar chase, letting the audience know from the get-go that this is not your typical "in-control" Bond. The effects of Bond's actions create ripples with his relationship with M and MI6; His carelessness leads to the death of Solange, an event that affects Bond emotionally, but one that he manages to internalize effectively --in what is essentially one of the best moments of Craig's acting--. Beyond the opening, Bond's ego leads him to lose everything during the Poker match with Le Chiffre, the eventual emotional fallout making him decide to assassinate Le Chiffre with a knife --an event prevented by the intervention of Felix Leiter--. And of course, the film reserves the biggest emotional punch for Bond in his relationship with Vesper Lynd.

Every action has a reaction that affects Bond and the world around him, and it is this exact narrative philosophy that makes characters interesting, engaging, and human. It is also what renders moments like the staircase fight, or the showdown in the Venice apartment in *Casino Royale* tenser. It is the essence of Fleming's Bond. Unfortunately, as Craig's tenure would continue, his Bond would progressively depart from this winning formula.

In what is essentially an epilogue to *Casino Royale*, 2008's *Quantum of Solace* continues some of the character fixtures that were established in Craig's first Bond outing. However, given the laser-focused approach on plot --as well as the reliance on the emotional events of the previous film-- *Quantum of Solace* fails to consistently place Bond in the same deep and contradicting emotional situations as in *Casino Royale*, opting for doubling down solely on the revenge aspect that the narrative calls for.

Situations such as Mathis' death and Bond's consolation of Camille over her fear of fire --while interesting-- fall flat given that the film does not present either a tonal or thematic counterpoint to the violent revenge-seeking Bond. *Casino Royale* uses subtle humor and some romantic and light-hearted elements to create said balance; deepening characters and their relationships in the process. *Quantum of Solace* skews that in favor of a more simplistic perspective on its characters --A baffling development given that 1989's *Licence to Kill* proved that a revenge-seeking Bond could work along with these balanced elements--. *Quantum of Solace* also introduces one of the key problems in Craig's tenure as Bond: The excessive psychoanalysis of the character.

While it does not reach the same heights as in 2015's *Spectre*, the seeds for this approach are sown with the way the filmmakers treat Bond's relationship with Vesper Lynd.

While the ghost of Vesper emotionally haunts Bond throughout the books, Fleming never portrays it in such an overt manner as in the films; Instead, Fleming chooses two poignant moments to throw in a reference in his usual succinct but impactful manner. The first instance of this can be seen in Fleming's *Goldfinger* novel, where a drugged Bond --believing that he had died and gone to heaven alongside Tilly Masterson-- makes the following reflection:

> "A deep fatherly voice said, almost in his ear, 'This is your captain speaking.' (Well, well. Who was this. Saint Peter?) We are coming in to land now. Will you please fasten your seat belts and extinguish your cigarettes. Thank you.' There must be a whole lot of them, going up together. Would Tilly be on the same trip? Bond squirmed with embarrassment. How would he introduce her to the others, to Vesper for instance?"

In his usual style, Fleming manages to make such a romantic thought feel melancholic, all thanks to the briefness of the mention, and the lack of extended pondering on behalf of Bond.

The second and final mention of Vesper can be found in the *On Her Majesty's Secret Service* novel. While *Goldfinger*'s reference is brief but touching, Fleming --and therefore Bond-- allows for a slightly more descriptive approach this time around. The intention is to bring finality to Vesper as an emotional demon to Bond; After all, this is the novel where Bond meets the second person to really enthrall and capture him emotionally since Vesper herself: Tracy.

As Bond arrives at Royale-les-Eaux --the place where the events of the *Casino Royale* novel took place--, Fleming writes:

> "James Bond idled through the pretty approaches to Royale, through the young beeches and the heavy-scented pines, looking forward to the evening and remembering his other annual pilgrimages to this place and, particularly, the great battle across the baize he had had with Le Chiffre so many years ago. He had come a long way since then, dodged many bullets and much death and loved many girls, but there had been a drama and a poignancy about that particular adventure that every year drew him back to Royale and its casino and to the small granite cross in the little churchyard that simply said 'Vesper Lynd. RIP.'"

Vesper --while an incredibly complex and compelling character in of herself--, is used by Fleming to provide the clearest examples of Bond's emotional processes. Bond never expresses his true feelings in public displays --like unbridled rage or crying--, the emotional tragedy of the character being the necessity to hold back and internalize his emotions because his life --and more often than not, the safe-keeping of his country and the world-- depends on it. As per Fleming's own philosophy on writing thrillers: If the hero is to save the world and get the girl, he's to suffer something in return.

With Craig's Bond, the filmmakers overplay the emotional angle to an ineffective extent. While the film adaptation of *Casino*

Royale provides a satisfactory pay-off and finality to Bond's relationship with Vesper, *Quantum of Solace* and --more egregiously-- *Spectre* continues to rope in Bond's relationship with Vesper as a constant, important, and all-encompassing mental tormentor to Bond. The unfortunate side-effect of this direction is that it retroactively cheapens the emotional complexity and impact of the character's relationship, since the contradictory nature of Bond's persona gets reduced to a single element, instead of the varying tensions that tug and pull at his psyche.

2012's *Skyfall* took a step forwards by eschewing the post-Casino Royale reliance on the Vesper arc; Instead choosing to explore Bond's relevancy in yet another differing socio-political context --one of increased techno-terrorism--, as well as his relationship to M and the Secret Service. While some ideas such as the expansion of Bond's relationship with M are interesting, the filmmakers place a heavy emphasis on Bond's psychology and abilities.

As previously mentioned, the entire first act of the film is dedicated to characters repeatedly questioning Bond's physical and mental ability --to the point that it becomes the centerpiece of almost every interaction--, and the film goes at length to repeatedly underline this fact by showcasing Bond struggling on his fitness test, his marksmanship test, and by having him partake in an overly-expository psychological cross-examination where his childhood trauma is laid out.

Beyond the first act, not only does villain Silva --played by Javier Bardem-- repeatedly teases and mocks Bond's psyche and emotional processes, he bases the entirety of his plan around Bond and M themselves --predicting their psychological responses to his advantage--; All while incessantly questioning Bond's relevance. Visually, the filmmakers continue to underline this theme with Bond's return to his Aston Martin DB5, as well as setting the climactic showdown not only on Bond's childhood home--Skyfall lodge--but more precisely at a chapel near the tombs of his dead parents.

Unfortunately, by revolving the plot and characters --and therefore the world of *Skyfall*-- exclusively around Bond, the film loses a lot of the emotional impact and complexity that was effective and welcomed in *Casino Royale.*

A key aspect as to what makes the character compelling is how Bond navigates his way around the world; How he reacts to it, and more often than not how he places himself in situations of difficulty and weakness, and whereas he succeeds --or fails-- to overcome them. *Skyfall* takes a completely different approach by making the Bond character the absolute center of everything in the film, numbing the audience to the effectiveness and consequentiality of his actions.

Comparing *Skyfall* to 1995's *Goldeneye* helps underline the narrative issues with the filmmakers' direction with Craig's Bond. As explored in the previous chapter, *Goldeneye* also concerns itself with Bond's relevancy in a radically different socio-political context, but unlike *Skyfall, Goldeneye* utilizes this key thematic element to its fullest potential, constructing an interesting, enveloping, and sinister Post-Cold War environment. Bond makes his way through a new world of changing allegiances --as seen in both his relationship with Trevelyan and Valentin Zhukovsky--, changing attitudes within the world of secret intelligence --as seen in his scenes with CIA agent Jack Wade, and by proxy in the scenes between Dimitri Mishkin and Orumov-- and last but not least, the overall changing cultural attitudes of the nineties --as seen in Bond's relationships with M, Moneypenny, and Natalya--.

In essence, instead of *telling* the audience about Bond's psyche and persona as *Skyfall* does, *Goldeneye shows* the audience what Bond's mental make-up is through his actions and decisions.

However, it is with 2015's *Spectre* that we find the most extreme and egregious examples of this overt psychoanalysis taken to its most absurd lengths.

The first --and the biggest-- narrative issue is the filmmaker's decision to rope in the events of all the Craig films under the Spectre banner. So as per the film, Le Chiffre, Mr. White, and Vesper from *Casino Royale*, Dominic Greene and the Quantum organization from *Quantum of Solace* and Silva from *Skyfall* are merely pawns and sub-sections to Spectre and Christoph Waltz's Blofeld.

In choosing this direction, the filmmakers retroactively devoid and minimize much of the events and emotional subtexts that the previous Craig films attempt to explore, and it renders much of the perceived impact and growth on the Bond character minimal and negligible --especially considering that the well-rounded and complex nature of *Casino Royale*'s Bond is streamlined to one or two emotional arcs by *Spectre*--. *Spectre* essentially places itself as a pay-off for a setup that was not there to begin with, and one that the same film forces in a very ham-fisted way; Distorting new and previously established character relationships in the process.

To add insult to injury, the nature of Blofeld vastly differs from his original incarnations in both the Fleming and the Connery Bonds. Instead of solely representing the world's most powerful, ingenious, and far-reaching criminal mastermind, the new Blofeld has a deeply personal relationship to Bond's past and repeatedly uses that to try to torment and attack him. More specifically, the fact that Blofeld's father took on a recently-orphaned Bond as his guardian, and Blofeld became jealous of his father's affections towards Bond.

Christoph Waltz's Blofeld not only represents a continuation of Bardem's Silva --in that he makes Bond's psychological torment his main personal quest--, it also is the final form of the overt psychoanalysis of the Bond character. The filmmakers zeroed in so much of the films around the psyche of Craig's Bond, that not only did they stunt the world around him --and Bond's relationship to it--, they also effectively neutered the two biggest threats to Bond and the world in the entire series: Blofeld and Spectre.

In trying to showcase emotional weakness on Bond's part -- and by progressively doubling down on a few characteristics instead of the character as a whole-- the filmmakers have accidentally made him so powerful that even Blofeld, the character that is supposed to represent the ultimate, cool-headed calculated evil genius, is emotionally reduced to simplified "daddy issues".

To further compound this, Bond manages to single-handedly destroy Spectre's secret lair in Morocco; All in a matter of minutes, and after going through Blofeld's torture --which was supposed to severely hamper his cognitive functions--.

The result is a film that is well made in a lot of aspects --and one that remains enjoyable for plenty of Bond fans--, but severely lacks the depth, suspense, and level of engagement that Craig's previous films had. Action set-pieces and character interactions lose all depth, tension, and suspense. *Spectre's* car chase through Rome does not feel as intense or consequential as the Madagascar chase, or even the opening train chase from *Skyfall*; Partly because the narrative up until this point starts running out of steam, but also because of some odd directorial choices: The streets of Rome are fully deserted during the chase, eliminating a layer of danger and tension that is present in the bustle of Istanbul in *Skyfall*'s opening chase, or the embassy in *Casino Royale*. Craig also seems to be merely mildly annoyed, and not even at the threat posed by Mr. Hinx --played by Dave Bautista--, but instead, at the lack of gadgetry present on his Aston Martin DB10.

Equally, Bond's relationship with Madeleine Swann is twisted and incongruent, with both characters declaring their love for each other only to have Madeleine suddenly want to separate from Bond in the next scene --with no narrative set-up nor emotional lead-up--. It is difficult to fully understand the direction the filmmakers want to take for their relationship given the shaky foundation it's built on.

In all, *Spectre* is the biggest example of the main issues with Craig's tenure. In deciding to depart from the formula set for *Casino Royale* --in essence, the Fleming formula--, the filmmakers ended up over-expanding and over-explaining a handful of characteristics of Bond's psyche, hampering Bond's relationship to the world, its characters, and therefore, himself; Even rendering him psychologically more powerful than a villain who is supposed to be his mental match. These problems, however, do not limit themselves to *Spectre*; With every post-*Casino Royale* Craig film either planting the seeds or carrying said issues progressively more to the forefront.

2021's *No Time To Die* will be Craig's final outing as Bond, and while it will, unfortunately, carry some of the baggage left over by *Spectre*, it will be the final point in what has been an incredibly successful and respectable tenure from Craig as James Bond. From box-office records to the love of the fans, Craig has managed to secure himself a very special place in the Bond pantheon as one of --if not-- the best Bonds of all time. Effectively harnessing the spirit of Fleming's Bond vision for 2006's *Casino Royale*, and introducing Fleming's Bond to yet another new generation and socio-political context. We can only then ask ourselves, what if the subsequent Craig Bond films had stuck to this formula?

PART III

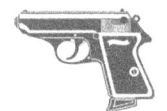

TIMOTHY DALTON

"You know, going in, that half the world loves Roger Moore and half the world loves Sean Connery. Whatever you do, you might end up with everybody in the world hating you." 39

-- TIMOTHY DALTON

With an aging Roger Moore out of the Bond role, and after the critical and commercial failure of 1985's *A View to a Kill*, Bond producer "Cubby" Broccoli decided to go for a radical change in the direction of the Bond films.

While at first toying with the idea of rebooting the franchise and exploring the Bond character from the beginning of his career as Secret Agent [40], the filmmakers decided instead to take a more serious approach and bring the character back to its literary roots; And after a brief contractual paroxysm that led to Pierce Brosnan losing out the role, Timothy Dalton was brought in to take on this new challenge.

This decision was in part sponsored and pushed by Dalton himself, who was an avid Fleming reader [41]. All of the sudden, Bond was back on a steady diet of Martinis and cigarettes, while once again being existentially stuck in his role as a reluctant hero who is not exactly at ease with his job. The attention to detail was such that Dalton's Bond --much like Fleming's vision of Bond-- kept his cigarettes in a sleek, gunmetal case; Only seen once in 1962's *Dr. No*, but a style staple of the literary version of the character.

However, this attention to detail was not limited to the appearance and aesthetics of the Bond character, it was extended to the world around him and the narratives themselves.

While still preserving a healthy amount of fantastical moments and set-pieces, Dalton's Bond concerned itself with very real and contemporary issues for the time. 1985's *The Living Daylights* can easily be considered the last true piece of Bond-related media directly correlated to the Cold War; With the film touching upon the Russian invasion of Afghanistan and the Mujahadeen, as well as the geopolitical tensions between East and West --after all, the film starts with a very crafty defection--. 1989's *Licence to Kill* deals with the cocaine cartel boom of the late eighties, complete with their intertwining with the power structures of both South and North America, and with villain Franz Sanchez almost being a sort of caricature of Pablo Escobar's perceived lifestyle and cruelty.

In doing this, the filmmakers rescue the Bond franchise from the self-spoofing realm that they found themselves in with Moore's Bond, and set the foundation for a more credible and serious approach for the character. In a way, it is a helpful framework for the writers to stick to the tone they want while the narrative is being developed.

With a more grounded, realistic, and fleshed-out world comes equally grounded, realistic and fleshed-out characters, with the most notable indicator of this being the female characters.

At a glance, we will find that Dalton is the Bond with the least amount of "conquests" --totaling three, the lowest of all Bond actors [42]. Limiting Bond to Maryam D'Abo's Kara Milovy, Carey Lowell's Pam Bouvier, and Talisa Soto's Lupe Lamora. This is not to say, however, that there is a loss of charm on behalf of Dalton; Instead, in reducing the amount of flings Bond has, more space is given to the female characters to develop their arcs.

The Bond girls in the Dalton films are not the typical throwaway eye candy audiences would normally find in a Connery or a Moore Bond film. Their respective roles in the narratives are prevalent and important, to the point that they finally offer a much-needed emotional counterpoint to Bond himself. This is a character philosophy that Fleming pursued for his books; After all, this is the impetus that created such memorable characters like Vesper Lynd and Tracy Di Vicenzo.

Dalton's Bond becomes more invested in his relationships with the female characters, and this allows for more impactful interactions, character growth, and conflict. In the case of *The Living Daylights*, Kara Milovy goes from naive cello virtuoso to a world-weary warrior woman --herself being the catalyst to a full-on Mujahadeen invasion on a Russian airfield--; And in the case of *Licence to Kill*, Pam becomes a barometer for the consequence of Bond's actions: While conducting an operation of her own against Sanchez, Bond's bloodlust for revenge costs her greatly, repeatedly jeopardizing her work --to the point of almost compromising Pam's CIA asset inside Sanchez's cartel: Heller--.

The female characters, however, are not the only ones that are given special attention. Villains and friends of Bond --for the most part-- receive the same treatment, with the most compelling example being Robert Davi's Franz Sanchez.

Charismatic, powerful, and cruel, Sanchez is introduced to the narrative of *Licence To Kill* in a spirit akin to the introduction of Blofeld and SPECTRE in the series: With the idea that his influence is far-reaching, being able to strike at the most unexpected of times. This is made evident with his escape from capture towards the beginning of the film, his treatment of Leiter, as well as MI6, the DEA, and CIA resisting the prospect of joining Bond on his assault at Sanchez.

His cartel, then, is presented as a highly organized, powerful, and efficient enterprise; However, this does not remain static throughout the narrative. As Bond manages to slowly infiltrate the cartel, he utilizes Sanchez's appraisal for loyalty against him, progressively turning Sanchez into an increasingly paranoid individual. The more Bond advances, the more Sanchez's influence and control diminish; The result is a desperate Sanchez retorting to violently silencing anybody that opposes him --as seen in him killing Truman-Lodge after repeated challenges to his authority--, and taking the risky decision to call-off his important drug deal with the Chinese in an attempt to salvage his cocaine tankers. Sanchez effectively undergoes a downwards spiral, thanks to Bond's --and his own-- actions. The consequentiality of said actions progressively ramps up the stakes, increases suspense, emotional tension --and therefore-- audience engagement.

The Living Daylights forgoes the singular charismatic villain, instead opting for a more specific group of people: Soviet general Georgi Koskov, his henchman Necros, and American arms dealer Brad Whitaker. While possessing quirks and eccentricity in their own right, the trio makes for some of the most realistic and down-to-earth Bond villains in the series.

Aside from being a necessity given the intent to stick to a more realistic context, this decision brings Bond closer to Fleming's vision; Since the literary version of the character mostly confronts Soviet spies pertaining to *Smiert Spionon* (Smersh), or other political operatives of the Cold War --with the only real "megalomaniac evil genius" types being Blofeld and Dr. No--. The decision to bring the political edge back to the forefront allows for the resurfacing of the moral throughline that Fleming set himself as a framework for the Bond series: that of the heroes and ideologies of today becoming the villains of tomorrow, and the moral ambiguity and allegiance-shifting of the intelligence world.

It is no coincidence that Koskov's plan to have Pushkin --his Soviet competition-- assassinated by the British Government plays on this exact sentiment. Pushkin, once seen as a friendly presence for the West inside the Soviet state apparatus, is suddenly seen as a threat to British national security. For M and the Minister of Defence, Pushkin goes from ally to a target to be eliminated. It is only with Bond, and the emotional tensions that reside within him, that we both see the moral contradiction to M's coldness, and the ruse that Koskov elaborates.

Brad Whitaker also operates on a similar level: a failed military career in America leads him to pursue his profession as an arms dealer, effectively arming the enemies of America's interests abroad. Fleming's moral throughline is also present in *Licence to Kill*: Killifer--one of Leiter's partners in the CIA-- is responsible for both Sanchez's escape and Leiter's maiming; SImilarly, Bond suspects that Pam is working undercover for Sanchez, something that emotionally discombobulates him.

Necros, in contrast to Koskov and Whitaker, is not a villainous representation of the moral ambiguity of politics and the intelligence world. Instead, Necros represents the flipside to the typical Bond henchman: that of a human being that happens to be effective at killing people. While henchmen like Oddjob or Jaws are striking in their physical presence, ruthlessness, and fantastical presentation, Necros is striking in how normal he is: The henchman is as human as Bond is --or the audience for that matter--. The fact that Necros begs Bond for mercy as he is about to be ejected to his death drives the point home.

Beyond villains, the emphasis on Bond's existential condition also extends to his co-workers. For the first time, Bond's relationship with M is repeatedly strained and contentious. In *The Living Daylights,* the envelope is pushed with Bond's skepticism over Pushkin's role in *Smiert Spionam,* to which an annoyed M threatens to take Bond out of the case, and even questions his ability to maintain a cool head. However, the extreme is reached with Bond's decision to go rogue in *Licence to Kill.* "Effective immediately, your license to kill is revoked" retorts M just after expressing his outrage at Bond's facile treatment of his actions so far. Being the maximum expression of his intelligence work, M becomes a big point of influence in regards to Bond's existential tension with his work. A relationship made explicit in *The Living Daylights* with Saunders. As Bond is being scolded by Saunders for disobeying a direct order --and running the risk of botching Koskov's defection--, he reacts directly and acidly: "Stuff my orders! [...] if M fires me I'll thank him for it". A sentiment never-before expressed by Bond in the film series, and one that finally places him as the reluctant hero he always was. The setup of Bond being dissatisfied with his job makes the death of Saunders and the maiming of Felix

Leiter all the more impactful for him --and the audience--. It lends a perspective of Bond as an almost Sisyphean figure, perpetually stuck in the intelligence game while in a futile chase to maintain his humanity.

The filmmakers, then, decided to return to Fleming for this new era of Bond. Bringing the franchise out of the fantastical heights of the Moore Bonds, and into the gritty of real-world politics and moral relativism. While doing so, they also focused on more refined and fleshed-out characters, relationships, and narratives. The world of James Bond would become more serious and sinister than what the audiences were used to, but it would also become more emotionally rich, textured, consistent --and therefore-- engaging. What remains is the one vital element that manages to connect everything effectively, and deliver a masterful adaptation of Bond: Timothy Dalton himself.

The first and most immediately noticeable trait of Dalton's performance is his physicality. Throughout the books, Fleming consistently describes Bond as having "dark, rather cruel good looks"; With characters --particularly Bond's female counterparts-- consistently noting Bond's "cruel mouth, and cold eyes". One cannot help but notice Dalton's ease in portraying Bond's cruelty and seriousness; Not just in the severity of his eyes, and the sharp factions of his face, but in his voice and delivery as well. Dalton portrays Bond's physicality exactly in the way Bond was intended to be: as a scalpel that can move in and out of the shadows, while donning the mask of a British gentleman.

Dalton never becomes a *bon vivant* in the way that Moore does, yet he looks at home in a social setting like a Casino or an Opera House; At the same time, he is not the brutish sledgehammer that Connery and Craig are, instead being always calculated, precise and dispassionate. A great example of Dalton's ability to tether the line between the internal coldness and the outwards projection of a gentleman can be found in *Licence To Kill*'s casino scene.

Bond attempts to gain Sanchez's attention by winning at a Blackjack table alongside Pam. Before long, Sanchez --who owns the Casino-- sends Lupe to substitute for the existing dealer and get more information on Bond. Once the dealers switch, Bond realizes his chance at an introduction, so he devises a distraction for Pam --who is posing as his secretary, Ms. Kennedy--.

"Ms. Kennedy, would you get me a medium-dry vodka Martini?" says Bond in an increasingly more direct and intense tone. As soon as Pam protests Bond's request, Dalton cuts her with a razor-sharp and cruel delivery of the iconic line: "Shaken, not stirred". The intensity of Dalton's delivery and the fact that the restrained vitriol is directed at a Bond girl is striking even to this day --even when used to Craig's brutishness in his performance--.

The method of delivery also packs a wealth of subtext on Bond's machinations. The dispassionate sentiment of Bond being on a mission, the same one that Connery delivers perfectly in his Bond performance, is present; After all, his objective is to meet Sanchez, and he will not let Pam get in the way. However, whereas Connery's Bond would stop there, Dalton's Bond has the added level of his internal emotional turmoil --his quest to avenge Leiter--. Bond's cold hatred for Sanchez is painfully evident; And whereas the filmmakers would possibly attempt to make Bond's emotion the entire centerpiece of the scene in the case of a Craig portrayal, for Dalton, the succinct yet direct nature of it --very much akin to Fleming's writing style-- packs a bigger punch, while at the same time subtly ramping the tension and suspense without overtaking the on-screen action.

Dalton's physical effectiveness does not limit itself to the social settings, he becomes an even bigger force to be reckoned with in the more violent and action-oriented scenes. This is something that is immediately established at the beginning of *The Living Daylights*. As Bond and Saunders prepare for the coming defection of Koskov, Dalton delivers the dispassionate ease that Bond has at the coming act of murder. The cold cruelty in his demeanor, his simple economy of movement, and the calmness of Dalton's delivery do not fail to underline the true essence of Bond in the most objective manner possible: At his core, Bond is a stone-cold killer. The presence of Saunders, a bureaucratic entity clearly on edge and anxious for the success of his mission, provides a contrast to Dalton's relaxed attitude. In its subtle way, this moment represents yet another instance of the different filmmaking departments working in perfect harmony to deliver a deep portrayal of Bond; One of the key ingredients being Saunders' presence as a grounding contradiction to the cruelty of Dalton's Bond.

A simpler scene where this becomes evident can be found in *Licence To Kill*. Bond infiltrates the WaveKrest and finds himself in Milton Krest's cabin --with the full intent of interrogating him, if not outright killing him--. He finds Lupe sleeping on his bed, and as she wakes up startled at Bond's presence, Dalton brutally silences her with his hand and places a knife up to her neck. Bond then delivers the line: "Make a sound, and you're dead" with such on-point seriousness that for the first time we believe that Bond would kill the Bond girl. A possibility only explored previously in Fleming's own *Live And Let Die* with Bond deciding to drown Solitaire before they get keelhauled over the reef. The scalpel-like danger of Bond becomes alive with Dalton's delivery.

Dalton also manages to deliver the action scenes throughout *The Living Daylights* and *Licence To Kill* with an added level of grit. Mainly because of his ability to perform his own stunts --very much like Craig would famously do after him--. Dalton's willingness to do so grants the filmmakers a much wider array of directorial choices for how to portray the action scenes.

In the hands of talented writers and directors, the action scenes obtain a real sense of danger no matter how fantastical the set-piece is; Because the illusion of realism becomes more palpable by seeing the actor being put in a physically demanding situation. Comparing the action scenes from Moore's Bond films from the eighties with Dalton's --all directed by John Glenn-- will immediately underline a difference in tension and suspense. Obviously, there are other narrative elements at play that dictate the effectiveness of the action set-pieces; But the ability to have the actor do his or her stunts unlocks a whole new level of potential for the filmmakers to exploit.

Apart from the sense of danger imbued by Dalton's willingness to perform his stunts, the action set-pieces are orchestrated with more consideration to Bond's realism as a character. Unlike his predecessor, the audience can get a real sense of Bond improvising his way through the action, and how oftentimes he is overwhelmed by the surrounding foes. In other words, Dalton's Bond often lacks *control* of many given situations, resulting in greater narrative tension for the action set pieces.

The perfect example of this impetus can be found in Bond's

escape from the Wavekrest in *Licence to Kill*.

The set-piece begins with a rash decision on behalf of Bond: He steps out into the open in order to immediately kill the person responsible for the death of his friend Sharkie. The act, borne out of pure emotion and irrationality, immediately places Bond in a situation of grave danger: He is greatly outnumbered and only has a knife to defend himself.

Bond immediately improvises and jumps into the water; taking the scuba gear from the man he just killed to gain some leverage over his situation.

As this is happening, a drug exchange is underway at the surface. With cocaine being loaded onto one of Milton Krest's robot submarines in exchange for packets of cash being loaded onto a seaplane. Through a series of carefully placed shot/counter-shots, Bond becomes aware --on the spot-- of how Sanchez's drug trafficking system works. Bond's immediate priority becomes to sabotage as much as he can of this exchange.

It is because of these close-ups that the psychology of the scene is set: Bond is improvising, he is *reacting* to the world around him.

Once the submarine is set to return to base, Bond immediately sets on to destroy the cocaine held within it. The decision places him at greater risk since by doing this, he renders himself visible to the team of WaveKrest divers that are chasing him.

By now, the divers have managed to catch up to Bond, and he is almost immediately overwhelmed by the group, and in one of the most surprising moments in the entire Bond film canon, the filmmakers decide to momentarily strip Bond of total control: He is swarmed, his oxygen line is severed and his scuba mask is immediately taken away from him. There are no Q gadgets to get him out of the situation, and the music swells to a shrill of maximum tension. Just as things appear to be lost for Bond, he manages to take a speargun from one of the divers and shoot it in a last-ditch attempt at the escaping seaplane; Dalton's face during the moment immediately communicates the element of desperation.

Thankfully for Bond, the spear lands on the plane, and he is quickly ejected away from the divers and into the surface. As he begins to ski his way to the seaplane, the music switches into a powerful rendition of the Bond theme. Bond eventually boards the plane, takes control of it, and escapes; Having narrowly avoided death, and having sabotaged Sanchez's all-important drug exchange.

The orchestration of the set-piece is precise in servicing both the narrative of the film and the Bond character. First, it sustains the key thematic element of Bond going rogue and facing Sanchez's cartel head-on, along with the full handicap of not counting on the resources of MI6 behind him. Secondly, and perhaps more importantly, it utilizes the on-screen action to portray the impulsive and emotional state of Bond --as well as his ability to overcome the situation at hand--.

Almost every decision that the character makes in the scene --and the rest of the film-- is borne out of the internal turmoil of his vendetta against Sanchez, as well as the frustration that neither the machinations of the DEA, CIA, or MI6 are willing to join him on his endeavors; A continuity of the key tension of emotion versus duty that is inherently important for the Bond character. The irrationality, however, constantly places him in ever-increasing danger --thus, ramping up the narrative stakes in the story--. Every decision that Dalton's Bond makes creates ripples throughout the rest of the narrative; The action set-pieces, then, manage to realize their full potential as tools for visual storytelling, *showing* the audience the nature of the characters and how they react to the world --much in a similar fashion to how an effective musical utilizes dance setpieces to *show* an aspect about its characters and their relationships--.

One of the most common criticisms levied at Dalton's performance is his perceived lack of humor. While a more modern audience --one that accepts and cherishes the style of Craig's Bond-- may find this to be an odd comment to underline, it makes perfect sense when seen in the context of the mid-eighties. After all, audiences became accustomed to fifteen years of Roger Moore's flippant style of performance as Bond.

For many, the Bond films became comedic action films for the whole family --a whole deviation from the intended targeted adult audience of both Fleming's Bond and the original Connery adventures--, so the audience shock of walking into Dalton's Bond with the pre-conceptions created by Moore's performances becomes more understandable. However, this is not to say that Dalton's Bond is completely devoid of any humor whatsoever; On the contrary, there is a healthy dose of humoristic and light-hearted elements to the character --after all, it is necessary to create the vital contradiction the characterization necessitates--.

Very much like Fleming did, the humor is present with subtlety and quickness; It never takes center stage in the narrative, nor do scenes exist solely to become punch-lines. Bond still preserves a sense of humor even in the most urgent and critical of times; As he places Koskov in the pipeline to the West --running the potential to turn him into "borscht" if Bond miscalculates the timing of the pressure release of the capsule--, he openly jokes at how he will be the first person to test the method of escape, comedically muffling the screams of a scared Koskov as he slams the capsule shut.

Another perfect example is Dalton's demeanor during the car chase from *The Living Daylights*. As Bond and Kara are making their escape to Austria, Bond utilizes the gadgets in his Aston Martin V8 to gain the upper hand on the pursuing KGB officers; A baffled and confused Kara repeatedly reacts to the uses of the gadgets.

As Bond's laser slices one of the KGB cars off its chassis, Kara quickly asks "what happened?", to which Bond replies --in a very ironic tone-- "salt corrosion". Throughout the rest of the chase, Dalton's Bond maintains this style of delivery with Kara, culminating in the most humoristic set-piece of Dalton's brief tenure as Bond: The snowy escape onboard Kara's cello case.

While *Licence to Kill* is gloomier and darker than *The Living Daylights*, humor is still very much present in the film. As Bond knocks out one of Dario's henchmen at a bar he is in with Pam, he quips to a waitress taking their orders: "He's had enough, run a tab". Bond is also cheerful and humorous during Leiter's wedding party, and there are some light-hearted moments alongside Q. "I hope you don't snore, Q" says Bond after realizing he will have to share a room with him.

It is certainly not the outrageous *Moonraker* style of humor that was consistent throughout the Moore Bond films, but it would be a stretch to say that Dalton's Bond is devoid of humor whatsoever. It is applied in concise and appropriate ways to create the tonal balance and emotional contradictions that make both the character of Bond and the world around him as compelling and rich as they should be.

While the majority of the elements that make Dalton's portrayal of Bond pitch-perfect are the result of the combined, harmonious efforts of the filmmakers towards the same goal, a lot needs to be said for Dalton's acting abilities.

In a previous chapter, we asked ourselves the central question --and challenge-- in adapting Bond to the big screen: "How do you outwardly perform the inner monologue of a cold, detached and gritty character?". Dalton manages to do so not with the stoicism of Connery or the comedy of Moore, nor the stunted emotion of Brosnan or the psychological overtness of Craig. Dalton's projection is that of a man wearing a cracked mask; A man that while struggling on the inside, remains seemingly cool-headed on the outside --save for the small fissures that merely give us a glimpse of his inner workings--. Dalton manages to deliver this not only with the more clear aspects of his physicality --his sharp features, cruel eyes, and severe cadence in his voice--, but also by adding enough subtleties in his facial expressions to bring the right dose of visual vulnerability hinted in the otherwise cruel face.

In *The Living Daylights,* we get a perfect example of this -- and probably one of the defining moments of Bond's characterization-- with the death of Saunders.

The film establishes Saunders' relationship with Bond from the very beginning as adversarial; The overly bureaucratic nature of Saunders grinding hard with the cruel killer instincts of Bond. "What's your escape route?" asks Bond as he is preparing his sniper rifle. "Sorry, old man." replies Saunders "Section 26, paragraph 5, that information is on a need-to-know basis only. I'm sure you'll understand".

After Koskov's defection and Bond's disobedience in failing to kill Kara, their subsequent interactions become more aggravated, with Saunders representing the very aspect of the job at hand that Bond himself is struggling with: the tension between his morality and humanity, and what the job calls for. It is this exact tension that prompts Bond to express his dissatisfaction with his occupation.

However, later in the film, as Bond invests himself in both Koskov's plot and Kara, he manages to meet Saunders again in Vienna --in order to obtain more information on Kara's cello, since it may provide a lead as to who is behind Koskov--. The ensuing interactions progressively equalize Saunders' and Bond's relationship. Saunders shows that he is comfortable straying away from the rules and the bureaucracy, while at the same time Bond shows a renewed commitment to the job at hand --which is essentially, Saunders' brainchild--.

The relationship reaches its peak as Saunders meets Bond at the Prater Cafe with the information necessary for Bond to proceed. In stark contrast to how the relationship is introduced at the beginning of the film, the two are --for the first time-- completely on the same page, with their body language finally suggesting ease at their mutual presence. Finally, the two of them operate at a level in which they both respect each other as intelligence agents.

Once the exchange is done, a happy-looking Saunders gives Bond a handshake as he says goodbye; But before he can leave the cafe, Bond stops him one more time to finally say "thank you". Dalton's face relaxes as he gives out a sigh of relief --the first time we see Bond at ease with a male counterpart instead of a female one--. Essentially, Bond is allowing himself the emotional comfort of knowing that he has someone on his side who is resourceful, reliable, and --perhaps more importantly-- friendly to him. Bond is letting his guard down.

As Saunders approaches the exit of the cafe, an explosive device planted by Necros detonates inside the mechanism of the cafe's automatic door system. The heavy glass and metal door collides with Saunders at a high speed. The glass shatters while Saunders falls to the floor, dead.

Bond, his face contorted in horror, runs to where Saunders' body lays, as the cafe patrons and onlookers all gather around the tragic scene. This is where Dalton's acting masterclass begins to show.

As he kneels, subtle tones of confusion and sadness are strewn on his face, clearly having difficulty digesting the shocking image he is seeing, and the emotional torment it causes him. At this moment, one can hear Fleming's words: "More blood!...More death!".

Before long, a lone balloon makes its way towards the scene. Bond takes a look at it in resignation; Dalton taking in a deep breath, anger slowly sweltering his face: the killer's signature, *Smiert Spionon*, is written on the balloon. The same signature found on the body of one of his double-o colleagues at the opening of the film.

Engulfed in impotent rage, Bond tightens the grip of his hands to the point of popping the balloon. Dalton widens his eyes and has them dart around ever-so-slightly while his jaw muscles tense. Bond, having emotionally lowered his guard mere moments before, struggles to internalize the emotions he feels.

As more people gather around the cafe, Bond sets his eyes on a set of balloons being carried by someone on the other side of a hedge.

Dalton's Bond immediately throws himself in desperate pursuit, even tripping as he starts running.

He then unholsters his Walther PPK, manages to get a jump at the person on the other side, and points the gun with the intent to shoot...

...Only to then reveal that it's a mother and her son walking with their balloons. Bond immediately holsters the gun in horror, realizing that he almost shot innocent civilians --including a child--.

Away from the cafe, and with Kara now on his side, Bond gives himself a moment to process his feelings. Kara then asks Bond about Koskov, immediately prompting Dalton to narrow his eyes and stare at Kara with a cold, hard stare of repressed cruelty and vitriol. Bond answers Kara's inquiry in an equally menacing voice --one that would be suited for a Shakespeare villain--.

And in a final masterstroke, he looks away from Kara and into the distance; Relaxing his face once again, accepting once again the realities of his existence with passive resignation.

Throughout the scene, the emotional core of Bond's character is laid bare for the audience to see: The build-up to a friendship with a colleague, with the eventual emotional acceptance of Saunders as a friend; Then the twist of fate and the emotional horror Bond has to face: suppress your humanity --your emotion-- or get eaten up in a world where the friends of today are the enemies of tomorrow. The eventual emotional load leads Bond to take an uncalculated and irrational decision, risking shooting a mother and a child in the process. Then the brutal internalization in front of his female counterpart, and then finally, ever so slightly, a small moment of reprieve for himself. Away from the other characters, but always present for the audience. Bond finally comes alive on the big screen.

While this may be the one overt moment in Dalton's tenure where the emotional and narrative effectiveness of a faithful Fleming adaptation is present, it is by no means the only one in all of Dalton's tenure as Bond.

Perhaps it is Bond's discovery of Leiter's maimed body in *Licence to Kill* that comes as a close second to Bond's reaction to Saunders' death. In this case, as Bond enters Leiter's office -- thrashed by Sanchez's men-- he sees on a nearby couch what is obviously Leiter's body wrapped in plastic. Dalton stops on his track to give himself a deep breath; His eyes give a very concise projection of his feelings: he is prepared to take in the horror to come.

Bond then calmly walks towards Leiter and begins unwrapping the plastic. He then sees Leiter's bloodied face, to which Dalton reacts with an exhale, a slight wandering of the eyes, and a tilt of the head; Communicating frustration and sadness on behalf of Bond. The frustration comes from either the powerlessness of Bond to do something about it, a reflection of the dangerous consequences of their jobs, or a combination of both. The delivery of Dalton also seems to suggest a bittersweet tenderness towards his long-time friend, the only time in the series where Bond concedes this much emotion to a male friend.

Bond's attention then turns to the note attached to Leiter, which reads: "He disagreed with something that ate him" --a reference to Leiter's maiming by a shark--. Dalton then, consumed once again by swelling anger, crumples the note and throws it away; All while his mouth quivers, and his eyes frown; trying to take in the cruelty of the action while at the same time preventing himself from outwardly displaying his emotions.

As soon as Leiter wakes up --calling for Della, his now-deceased wife-- Bond is snapped into his on-the-job survival mode, effectively providing the needed catalyst to help Bond internalize his emotions. The phone then rings, and Bond is able to call for help.

The complex mix of emotions, expertly delivered with the necessary subtlety by Dalton, lends an exceptionally tragic light to the scene that goes beyond the maiming of a beloved friend of Bond --and a defining character of the series as a whole--. The emotional tension of the risks of the job versus Bond's human need for emotion is present and palpable, and it provides the perfect set-up for Bond's plan of revenge, and the wealth of irrational and risky mistakes that he makes along the way.

When we compare this scene with its literary version -- found in Fleming's 1954 novel *Live And Let Die*-- we see Fleming's language flourish on the screen, as well as the emotional subtext it carries with it:

> *"With the movements of a sleep-walker, Bond put the piece of paper down on the bedside table. Then he turned back to the body on the bed. He hardly dared touch it for fear that the tiny fluttering breath would suddenly cease. But he had to find out something. [...] Soon he uncovered some of the strands of hair. [...] He pulled out some strands of hair and looked closely at them. There was no more doubt."*

The bittersweetness, the powerlessness, and the inevitable emotional repression of Bond are felt throughout Fleming's writing and Dalton's performance. Bond's fear of touching Leiter's body for fear of hurting him is echoed in Dalton's delicateness and facial expressions when uncovering the plastic. The sleep-walker-like movement described by Fleming finding its way through Dalton's calm-yet-defeated walk towards Leiter.

Fleming continues:

> *"He saw again the pale straw-coloured mop that used to hang down in disarray over the right eye, grey and humorous, and below it the wry, hawklike face of the Texan with whom he had shared so many adventures. He thought of him for a moment, as he had been. Then he tucked the lock of hair back into the bandages and sat on the edge of the other bed and quietly watched over the body of his friend and wondered how much of it could be saved."*

While slightly more ponderous than its on-screen counterpart, the essence of the scene is perfectly captured. Fleming's succinct mention of Bond thinking of Leiter as "the Texan with whom he had shared so many adventures with" is perfectly summarized by Dalton in his reaction when uncovering the plastic from Leiter and seeing his face; The internal monologue is perfectly seen by the audience, but it is never overplayed or over-emphasized.

Equally, Bond thinking of how much of Leiter can be saved --if anything at all-- can be seen after Dalton crumples the note; As his eyes frown and his mouth quivers, he quickly examines the body from head-to-toe, in no doubt assessing the damage on

Leiter's body, seeing what can be saved.

These two instances --Saunders' death and the discovery of Leiter's maimed body--, are the two most perfect examples of Dalton's effectiveness at portraying the character of James Bond, with the result being the creation of an extremely deep, engaging, and emotionally textured rendition of the characters.

This depth and texture extend to the characters surrounding him, their relationships, and the world of Bond overall. All thanks also in part to the conscious decision of the filmmakers to bring Bond back to his literary roots.

Effectively, while heavily underrated for the time, *The Living Daylights* and *Licence To Kill* provide the most complete and impactful portrayals of James Bond since Fleming himself committed the character to the page from 1953 up until his untimely death in 1964.

It would take seventeen years, with the release of 2006's *Casino Royale*, for the audience to get yet another complete look at the original characterization of James Bond. This time though, said characterization was received with near-unanimous acclaim, a far cry from the luke-warm and down-right hostile reception Dalton received in the late-eighties.

In a way, a positive side-effect of *Casino Royale* and Craig's performance is that in introducing Fleming to the twenty-first century, Dalton's performance has been redeemed in the eyes of the modern audience, as evidenced in a 2020 poll run by popular UK magazine RadioTimes, where fans were asked to vote on who they considered to be the best Bond actor. Dalton arrived in a surprising second place with thirty-two percent of the votes, only being beaten by Sean Connery, who garnered forty-four percent of the votes [43]

Whether the popularity of Dalton's Bond will increase or decrease over the coming years remains to be seen, But one factor remains constant and proved: Dalton's Bond was simply ahead of its time.

CONCLUSION

"My feeling is this will be the last one. I don't mean my last one. I mean the end of the whole lot. I don't speak with any real authority, but it's sort of a feeling I have. Sorry!" 44

-- TIMOTHY DALTON

Coming off the lukewarm reception and commercial failure of *Licence to Kill* in the United States, the Bond team quickly got to work on what would have been Dalton's third Bond film. A seventeen-page treatment written by Michael G. Wilson and Alfonse M. Ruggiero became the starting point for the project, with the story concerning Bond's investigation into Hongkonger businessman Sir Henry Lee-Chin following a terrorist attack on a Scottish nuclear facility.

Before long, the project would be ground into an involuntary halt, and enter development hell.

In 1990 --shortly before Dalton's third Bond adventure was slated to begin production-- Metro-Goldwyn Mayer, the parent company of Bond film distributors United Artists, and producer "Cubby" Broccoli's company Danjaq --the intellectual property holders of the Bond series-- entered a three-year-long legal conflict over the television distribution rights for the Bond franchise.

The conflict lasted from 1990 until late-1993, effectively running through the remaining duration of Dalton's contract as James Bond.

To make matters worse, the Cold War would end in 1991 following the dissolution of the USSR. The world was suddenly thrown into a whole new political, social and cultural context very much unlike what nations were used to for over forty-five years. With this seismic cultural change, the poor box-office performance of *Licence to Kill,* the long gap between films, and the meddling popularity of Dalton as a Bond actor, the relevancy and profitability of the Bond franchise was suddenly faced with intense skepticism; With the Wall Street Journal calling the production of the new Bond film "A fifty-million dollar gamble that is not worth taking." [45]

With the easing of the legal issues in 1993, the filmmakers decided to proceed with a brand-new script written by Michael France --*Goldeneye*-- by the end of the year. However, with all the lost time having passed by, Dalton was only intending to do one more film, while producer Broccoli stressed that given the gap between *Licence to Kill* and *Goldeneye*, Dalton needed to participate in at least three or four more films.

While Dalton agreed with Broccoli's expectation, he felt he could not commit to appearing in more than one film. And in April 1994, Timothy Dalton would officially walk away from the role. [46] Later that year, Pierce Brosnan would be announced to take on the

Bond role.

It is interesting to think how different the history of the franchise would have been if Dalton would have had the chance to make his third Bond outing. Would he have finally gained the acceptance of the public? Or would the series have died with him there and then?

Regardless of the outcome, Dalton's Bond tenure has had a considerable impact on the franchise's history; One akin to the Bond-mania that came after the release of 1964's *Goldfinger*, the massive success of 1977's *The Spy Who Loved Me*, and the Bond resurgence that came with 1995's *Goldeneye*. For the first time, Bond surpassed the existential confinement of being a pop-culture quasi-superhero; Becoming the flawed, brutal, and deeply human anti-hero of the Fleming novels.

This franchise-first move towards the more serious and grounded Fleming-Esque films would pave the way to the massively successful current run of films starring Daniel Craig as Bond, heralding the most lucrative and popular decade in the history of the Bond franchise. The success, in turn, has re-cast Dalton's Bond in an increasingly positive light in the eyes of modern audiences, with more and more people agreeing that Timothy Dalton was indeed the best Bond.

ENDNOTES

[1] Roger Ebert (17 November 1995). "GoldenEye". *Chicago Sun-Times*.

[2] James Berardinelli (1995). "GoldenEye". *Reelviews.net*.

[3] Groen, Rick (14 July 1989). "Licence to Kill". *The Globe and Mail*.

[4] Sarris, Andrew. "New Bond's Stormy Virility Trumps Connery and Moore". *The New York Observer*. 27 Nov. 2006

[5] Smith, Jim (2002). *Bond Films*. London: Virgin Books. ISBN 978-0-7535-0709-4.

[6] Duncan, Paul. *The James Bond Archives*, 1st ed., Taschen, 2012, pp-49.

[7] Barnes, Alan; Hearn, Marcus (1997). *Kiss Kiss Bang! Bang!: the Unofficial James Bond Film Companion*. Batsford Books.

[8] Malcolm, Derek, 16 December 1969. "Off the peg Bond". *The Guardian*.

[9] Zec, Donald, 16 December 1969. "Big film ... small fry". *Daily Mirror*.

[10] *Inside On Her Majesty's Secret Service* (DVD). *OHMSS* Ultimate Edition DVD: MGM Home Entertainment Inc. 2000.

[11] "Latest 007 Seeking to End His Bondage", *Los Angeles Times*, 24 November 1969, pg. 2.

[12] Riley, Stevan, director. *Everything or Nothing: The Untold Story of 007*. Sony Pictures Releasing, 2012.

[13] Barnes, Alan; Hearn, Marcus (2001). *Kiss Kiss Bang! Bang!: the Unofficial James Bond Film Companion*. Batsford Books.

[14] "Australian Non-Actor Chosen to Play James Bond". *The Washington Post, Times Herald*. 9 October 1968. p. D14.

[15] Barnes, Alan; Hearn, Marcus (1997). *Kiss Kiss Bang! Bang!: the Unofficial James Bond Film Companion.* Batsford Books.

[16] Block, Alex Ben; Autrey Wilson, Lucy (2010). *George Lucas's Blockbusting: A Decade-by-Decade Survey of Timeless Movies Including Untold Secrets of Their Financial and Cultural Success.* London: HarperCollins.

[17] "Diamonds Are Forever (1971) - Financial Information". *The Numbers*

[18] *Inside Live and Let Die: Live and Let Die Ultimate Edition, Disc 2* (DVD). MGM/UA Home Video. 2000. ASIN: B000LY209E.

[19] Riley, Stevan, director. *Everything or Nothing: The Untold Story of 007.* Sony Pictures Releasing, 2012.

[20] "James Bond Movies at the Box Office". *Box Office Mojo.*

[21] "Never Say Never Again". Nash Information Services, LLC. Retrieved 1 September 2011.

[22] Jeffrey, Morgan. "Sean Connery Named the Best James Bond after Thousands of 007 Fans Vote in Poll." *Radio Times*, ww.radiotimes.com/movies/sean-connery-best-james-bond-poll

[23] Benson, Raymond (1988). *The James Bond Bedside Companion.* London: Boxtree Ltd.

[24] Stockdale, Charles, and John Harrington. "Every James Bond Film Ranked From Worst to Best." *USA Today*, Gannett Satellite Information Network. https://www.usatoday.com/story/life/movies/2018/06/18/james-bond-every-007-film-ranked-worst-best/711547002/

[25] Lyttelton, Oliver. "Skyfail: The 5 Worst James Bond Films." *IndieWire*, 7 Nov. 2012, https://www.indiewire.com/2012/11/skyfail-the-5-worst-james-bond-films-104366/

[26] "Every James Bond Film Ranked from Worst to Best." *The Independent*, 22 Jan. 2021, https://www.independent.co.uk/arts-entertainment/films/features/james-bond-films-list-best-worst-007-ranking-no-time-to-die-delay-a9377531.html

[27] Suszczyk, Nicolas. *The World of Goldeneye: A Comprehensive Study on the Seventeenth James Bond Film and its Legacy.* 1st ed., Independent Publishing, 2019.

[28] "Box Office History for James Bond Movies". *The Numbers*. Nash Information Service.

[29] "2002 Yearly Box Office Results". *Box Office Mojo*.

[30] CrimeReads. "The Time Raymond Chandler and Ian Fleming Got Together To Talk About Thrillers." *CrimeReads*, 26 Oct. 2018, https://crimereads.com/the-time-raymond-chandler-and-ian-fleming-got-together-to-talk-about-thrillers/

[31] "Shaken Not Stirred: Selling a Super Spy." *BBC News*, BBC, 19 Nov. 1999, http://news.bbc.co.uk/2/hi/special_report/1999/11/99/shaken_not_stirred/525210.stm

[32] Roger Moore (4 October 2008). "Bye-bye to Ian Fleming's James Bond?". *The Times*. London.

[33] "**Biography: Timothy Dalton**". IanFleming.org. Archived from the original on 13 December 2002.

[34] Sterngold, James (30 March 1999). "Sony Pictures, in an accord with MGM, drops its plan to produce new James Bond movies". *The New York Times*.

[35] Desowitz, Bill. *James Bond Unmasked*. Published by Charles Helfenstein, 2012.

[36] "The Name's Bland.. James Bland". *Daily Mirror*. UK. 15 October 2005.

[37] La Monica, Paul R. (6 November 2006). "Blond, James Blond". CNN.

[38] "All-Time Worldwide Box Office Grosses". Box Office Mojo.

[39] Riley, Stevan, director. *Everything or Nothing: The Untold Story of 007*. Sony Pictures Releasing, 2012.

[40] Desowitz, Bill. *James Bond Unmasked*. Published by Charles Helfenstein, 2012.

[41] "Timothy Dalton on Penny Dreadful, Serenading Mae West, and Being James Bond." *TV Club*, 9 May 2014, https://tv.avclub.com/timothy-dalton-on-penny-dreadful-serenading-mae-west-1798269770

[42] "Booze, bonks and Bodies." *The Economist*, https://www.economist.com/books-and-arts/2012/10/20/booze-bonks-and-bodies

[43] Jeffrey Morgan. "Sean Connery Named the Best James Bond after Thousands of 007 Fans Vote in Poll." *Radio Times*, www.radiotimes.com/movies/sean-connery-best-james-bond-poll/.

[44] 2016, MI6-HQ. "Bond 17." *MI6: The Home of James Bond*, https://www.mi6-hq.com/sections/articles/bond_17_intro.php3

[45] Riley, Stevan, director. *Everything or Nothing: The Untold Story of 007*. Sony Pictures Releasing, 2012.

[46] Meslow, Scott. "Timothy Dalton Opens up about Penny Dreadful, Leaving James Bond, and the Demon in All of Us." *The Week*, 12 May 2014, https://theweek.com/articles/447045/timothy-dalton-opens-about-penny-dreadful-leaving-james-bond-demon-all

ABOUT THE AUTHOR

Diego Marquez

About The Author Diego Marquez Award-winning filmmaker and film analyst from Caracas, Venezuela. His cinematic essays especialize on the filmmaking process, as well as the historical and cultural impact of film in society.

For more information, visit diegomt.com/start

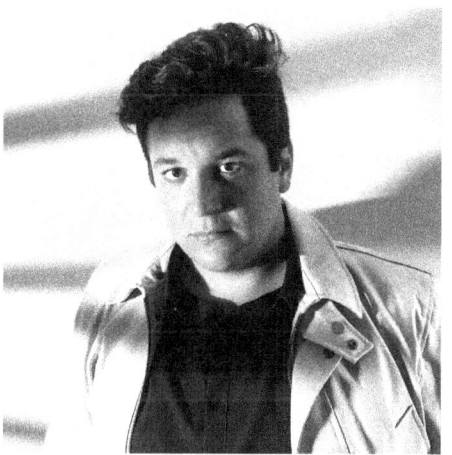

www.ingramcontent.com/pod-product-compliance
Lightning Source LLC
Chambersburg PA
CBHW050010230526
45465CB00003BB/1347